WIFE
RAPE

Sage Series on Violence Against Women

Series Editors

Claire M. Renzetti
St. Joseph's University

Jeffrey L. Edleson
University of Minnesota

In this series. . .

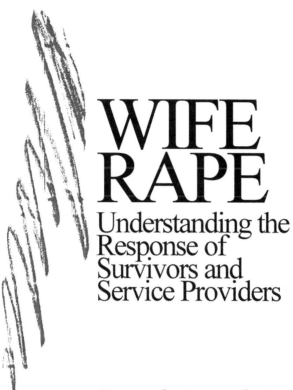

WIFE RAPE

Understanding the Response of Survivors and Service Providers

Raquel Kennedy Bergen

Sage Series on Violence Against Women

SAGE Publications
International Educational and Professional Publisher
Thousand Oaks   London   New Delhi

For information address:

 SAGE Publications, Inc.
2455 Teller Road
Thousand Oaks, California 91320
E-mail: order@sagepub.com

SAGE Publications Ltd.
6 Bonhill Street
London EC2A 4PU
United Kingdom

SAGE Publications India Pvt. Ltd.
M-32 Market
Greater Kailash I
New Delhi 110 048 India

Printed in the United States of America

Library of Congress Cataloging-in-Publication Data

Bergen, Raquel Kennedy.
   Wife rape: Understanding the response of survivors and service providers / author, Raquel Kennedy Bergen.
       p.   cm.—(Sage series on violence against women; v. 2)
   Includes bibliographical references and index.
   ISBN 0-8039-7240-7 (acid-free paper). — ISBN 0-8039-7241-5 (pbk.: acid-free paper)
       1. Rape in marriage—United States.   2. Rape in marriage—United States—Case studies.   3. Abused wives—United States—Case studies.
   4. Abused wives—Services for—United States.   I. Title.
   II. Series.
   HV6561.B48   1996   96-4426

This book is printed on acid-free paper.

02 01 00   10 9 8 7 6 5 4 3

Sage Production Editor: Diana E. Axelsen
Sage Typesetter: Andrea D. Swanson

Contents

Acknowledgments

I want to take this opportunity to express my sincere gratitude to the many people who were involved in the production of this book. First and foremost, I would like to thank the 40 survivors of wife rape who shared their stories with me. Although they must remain anonymous, I am forever grateful to them for their honesty and courage in speaking out about their painful experiences. I want them to know that their voices have been heard.

I am also grateful to the directors and staff members of the battered women's shelter and rape crisis center where I studied for speaking freely with me about their work and their interaction with wife rape survivors. Special thanks to the direct service coordinator for her assistance in recruiting study participants. Thanks also to those service providers nationwide who completed my survey and those who sent notes of encouragement. I am grateful to the Board on Faculty Research at St. Joseph's University, which provided me with a grant that made it possible for me to conduct the survey of service providers and finish writing this book.

I am particularly grateful to those who have provided me with support and encouragement during both my data collection and my writing. Special thanks to my graduate assistant, Gina Hackett, who went above and beyond the call of duty in helping with the library research, survey, and data analysis. I also appreciate the help of Denise

Shaw, who compiled Appendix A, and the efforts of Erin McKenna and Bridget Mason, who helped in disseminating the survey.

Charles Bosk, Demie Kurz, and Robin Leidner were invaluable sources of support, and their critical insights have, I hope, made this a better book. George Dowdall was helpful in lending encouragement when the end seemed nowhere in sight. I owe a particular debt of gratitude to Vicki Smith for her unfailing support, patience, and intellectual guidance through every stage of the research process. My comparative analysis of two women's agencies might not have been complete without her assistance. Thanks also to Jerry Jacobs, Elijah Anderson, and the anonymous reviewers of *Violence Against Women* and the American Sociological Association, who offered important critiques of earlier drafts. I am grateful to Laura X, director of the National Clearinghouse on Marital and Date Rape, who for more than 7 years has been providing me with assistance based on her expertise and resources. Thanks also to attorney John Bergen, who provided important legal information about wife rape. Special thanks to Terry Hendrix of Sage Publications for his guidance and support of this project. I am particularly grateful to Claire Renzetti—my colleague, friend, and editor— for her encouragement on this project and for her editorial expertise.

This book could not have been written without the emotional support of my friends and family. My dear friend, Cheryl Sloan Boyd, has offered continual encouragement of my work and served as a wonderful sounding board for my ideas. I am especially grateful to my family for their patience and understanding. My labradors, Kona and Huey, laid patiently at my feet while I wrote "just one more paragraph." Thanks to my son, Michael Ryan, who (almost) waited until this book was complete to be born. Finally, I owe the largest debt of gratitude to my best friend and husband, Michael, who has provided me with unending encouragement and support as I have struggled with this topic through the years. He has listened to me talk endlessly about wife rape, has read and reread every draft of every chapter, and has provided me with constant nurturance. For his loving support, I am thankful.

Preface

I first became interested in the subject of wife rape more than 7 years ago when, as an undergraduate, I was required to write a senior thesis on a topic of my choosing. At a total loss, I scanned the Sociological Abstracts and saw one listing for marital rape. When I began checking for other sources of information, I found only a handful. I quickly learned that there was a dearth of information on this subject not only in academic circles, but also among practitioners. For my senior thesis, I interviewed a dozen service providers and learned that not only did most of them lack information about wife rape, but some were downright hostile about the subject. My interest in wife rape continued throughout my graduate career, as I volunteered with various battered women's shelters and rape crisis centers. Countless numbers of women informally shared with me their personal stories of the pain and anguish they had suffered at the hands of their partners. Others allowed me to interview them formally, with the hope that their voices would be heard and that others would come to understand their trauma.

This book is an attempt to fulfill their hopes. In writing it, I share with you the stories of 40 women who were raped by their partners. Their words have been reproduced with only minor editing to preserve their anonymity and correct grammatical errors. I discuss their experiences of sexual violence, their efforts to get help from service providers, and the results of those efforts. Most of the women were dissatisfied with the assistance they received.

This book is not an effort to condemn the work of those involved in the battered women's movement and the anti-rape movement. Such work is invaluable and essential for the eventual elimination of violence against women. However, I will argue that the problem of wife rape has not received the attention it deserves within these movements and that the needs of an important group of women—wife rape survivors—have not been met. One of my goals in writing this book is to draw further attention to this important issue and indicate ways in which service providers can better help these women (again using their own words).

In writing this book, I hope to reach a wide variety of people. Certainly, my hope is that other survivors of wife rape will see their own stories in the experiences of the women who are presented here. I want them to know that they are not alone in their trauma, that their experiences are "really rape," and that they, too, can end the violence. It is also my hope that a variety of service providers, including battered women's shelter workers, rape crisis counselors, therapists, police officers, and religious leaders, will read this book and develop a better understanding of the serious problem of wife rape and how they can assist survivors of this form of violence.

This book is dedicated to the women
who shared their stories with me and
to all survivors of wife rape.

1

An Introduction to the Problem of Wife Rape

It was very clear to me. He raped me. He ripped off my pajamas, he beat me up. I mean some scumbag down the street would do that to me. So to me it wasn't any different because I was married to him, it was rape—real clear what it was. . . . I guess I can't say I would have been more fearful with a stranger because I didn't know when he was going to stop or if he was going to kill me. I never knew when he would stop beating me either. He would just stop when he got tired or whatever.

Karen

There needs to be somewhere for these women [survivors of wife rape] to go. I've been screwed by every agency in the area. This is a crime, no matter if your husband does this or not. Nobody has the right to drag me by my hair into the room and do that. There's such embarrassment and degradation you go through because you're a wife and some stranger didn't do it. It goes beyond the word *callous*—how people treat you. And you don't know where to go for this type of a problem. You can't get help and women need help. They need to know this is a crime and help those like me who were isolated—so isolated he wouldn't let me leave the house.

Wanda

This book is about the problem of wife rape. These quotations, taken from interviews with survivors of wife rape, provide answers to the two most important questions that have guided my research.[1] First, how do women understand and define their experiences of wife rape? Second, what is the response of agencies to women who seek their help?

As other researchers have established, wife rape is a very serious problem. An estimated 14% to 25% of women experience forced sex at least once during their marriages (Resnick, Kilpatrick, Walsh, & Veronen, 1991; Russell, 1990). Rape in marriage may well be the most common form of sexual assault, particularly if we consider that women who are involved in physically violent relationships may be especially vulnerable to being raped by their partners (Browne, 1993; Campbell, 1989; Russell, 1990; Walker, 1979). Research indicates that between one third and one half of battered women are raped by their partners and that sexual abuse is characteristic of the most violent relationships (Campbell, 1989; Hanneke, Shields, & McCall, 1986; Pagelow, 1992).

My intent in writing this book is not to contribute to knowledge about the prevalence of wife rape (for this, see Diana Russell's 1990 work[2]) but to provide a much needed analysis of how women experience wife rape and the response of institutions to women's help-seeking behavior. This analysis is shaped by my interviews with 40 survivors of wife rape and 37 service providers, my participant observation at a rape crisis center and battered women's shelter, and a survey of women's agencies in the United States. My hope is that service providers, as well as a variety of other interested people, will better understand the serious problem of wife rape after reading this book.

A Brief Legal History of Wife Rape

Thirty years ago, the topic of wife rape would not have been the focus of a scholarly paper, much less a book. Indeed, it is only recently that the United States has acknowledged that a man can be prosecuted for raping his wife. In the United States, as well as most other societies,[3] a husband could not be legally sanctioned for raping his wife until quite recently. This "marital rape exemption" still influences sexual assault legislation.

Russell (1990) argues that the origin of the marital rape exemption was the social understanding that women were the property of men, first of their fathers and then of their husbands. This is reflected in the first law of marriage decreed by Romulus of Rome in the 8th century B.C., a law that "obliged married women, as having no other refuge, to conform themselves entirely to the temper of their husbands and the husbands to rule their wives as necessary and inseparable possessions" (Sonkin, 1987, p. 6). Thus, with marriage, women became the property of their husbands.

The treatment of women as property is particularly evident when we examine the history of rape legislation. Rape laws were originally enacted as property laws, to protect a man's property (a daughter or a wife) from other men, not as laws to protect women or their rights to control their bodies (Pagelow, 1984). Thus, the penalty for rape was intended to punish a man for defiling another man's property. If a daughter was raped, her father could be compensated for the loss of his valuable property—his daughter's virginity. A husband could also be compensated for the violation of his sexual property if his wife was raped by another man. However, as owners of this property, husbands could not be charged with the rape of their wives (Dobash & Dobash, 1979).

This ideology was reinforced by the statements of Sir Matthew Hale, Chief Justice in 17th-century England. Hale's dictum, based on the notion of women as sexual property, is the foundation for the current marital rape exemption (Brownmiller, 1975). In the *History of the Pleas of the Crown,* published in 1736, Hale wrote, "The husband cannot be guilty of a rape committed by himself upon his lawful wife, for by their mutual matrimonial consent and contract, the wife hath given up herself in this kind unto the husband which she cannot retract" (quoted in Russell, 1990, p. 17).

In this pronouncement, Hale (a known misogynist who burned women at the stake as witches; Finkelhor & Yllö, 1985) argued that marriage implies an irrevocable consent to sex (Russell, 1990). By his reasoning, once married, a woman does not have the right to refuse sex with her husband for any reason. Furthermore, even if a woman had possessed the right to refuse intercourse, under British common law, she would have had no legal recourse to accuse her *husband* of rape because of the principle of matrimonial unity.

Reflecting this principle, legal thinker William Blackstone wrote in the late 1760s that "by marriage the husband and wife are one person in law; that is, the very being or legal existence of the woman is suspended in marriage" (Dobash & Dobash, 1979, p. 60). Once married, a wife's identity became legally merged with her husband's; she was not able to own property, have custody of children, or file charges against him. Accusing her husband of rape would have been impossible, because when her husband raped her, he was in effect raping himself, which was not plausible (Barshis, 1983; Turetsky, 1981). Clearly, with marriage, a husband gained a sexual title to his wife and an exemption from the charge of rape.

Until recently, this notion of sexual entitlement in marriage was largely accepted by U.S. courts. For example, in 1952, the Corpus Juris Secundum read, "Rape cannot be committed by a husband on his wife, either because such intercourse is not considered unlawful or because by marriage she consents to the intercourse with her husband, which [permission] she cannot withdraw" (quoted in Astor, 1974, p. 78).

These archaic understandings of rape were challenged in the 1970s, when the women's movement argued for the elimination of the spousal exemption in rape legislation (Bidwell & White, 1986). In 1978, John Rideout became the first man in the United States to be prosecuted for a rape he committed on his wife while he was living with her (Russell, 1990). Since this time, significant advances have been made in repealing state spousal exemptions from rape prosecution, using the argument that the exemptions do not provide all women with equal protection from rape (see *People v. Liberta* [Finkelhor & Yllö, 1985]). In particular, Laura X, the director of the National Clearinghouse on Marital and Date Rape, and other concerned feminists have been campaigning for changes in federal and state laws, the military code, and the laws of other countries.

In the United States, raping one's wife is now a crime in all 50 states, according to at least one section of the sexual offense codes. However, in 33 of these states, husbands are still exempt from prosecution in some situations.[4] (See Appendix C, "State Law Chart.") Ironically, in most of these states, a husband is exempt if his wife is vulnerable and unable to consent because she is mentally or physically impaired, unconscious, or asleep (Russell, 1990). This exemption indicates that a husband is entitled to take unfair advantage of his wife when she is helpless to defend herself.

Although there have been some important changes in the legal status of wife rape, the marital exemption has not been stricken from rape laws across the board. It is essential to do this, for as Pagelow (1984) notes,

> As long as husbands can rape wives with impunity from the law—
> women do not own their bodies. Striking the marital *privilege to rape*
> will be a signal to some possessive and violent men that their wives
> are not their property. (p. 423)

The current existence of spousal exemptions to rape under certain circumstances perpetuates the problem of wife rape because it allows individuals to believe that this behavior is somehow acceptable. Furthermore, it indicates the prevalence of the social understanding that women are still the property of their husbands and that the marriage contract is an entitlement to sex (Russell, 1990). The criminalization of wife rape under all circumstances is a necessary step toward eliminating this heinous crime.

Public Attention and Wife Rape

Given the legal ambiguity of wife rape, it is not surprising that there has been little popular discussion of wife rape in the United States. My review of the *Reader's Guide to Periodical Literature* reveals that, prior to 1971, there was little information on sexual assault in general and virtual silence on the specific topic of wife rape. The first article to appear in a popular magazine was titled "Legal Rape" and appeared in *Family Circle* in 1979 (Russell, 1990). Between 1979 and 1992, articles on wife rape appeared sporadically and focused primarily on state legislative changes. Between 1993 and 1994, the number of articles in popular journals increased (to a total of 27), largely as a result of the infamous case of John and Lorena Bobbitt.

Three cases of wife rape have received a relatively significant amount of press coverage in the United States. John Rideout was the first man to be criminally prosecuted for raping his wife while they were living together. The case of John and Greta Rideout drew a great deal of media attention and eventually became the basis for a television movie. This case was notorious because John Rideout was acquitted, and shortly thereafter, the Rideouts publicly announced their reconciliation (Russell, 1990). However, the media paid scant attention when Greta finally escaped John's violence, and he was convicted of several charges, including harassment. The media coverage of this case contributed to the popular perception that wife rape is not a serious offense.

In 1992, the media focused on a second case of wife rape. In South Carolina, Trish Crawford claimed that her husband, Dale, tied her to their bed, terrorized her with a knife, and raped her. The case went to trial, and the prosecution felt that their case was strong because Dale Crawford had videotaped the scene. However, Crawford was acquitted by a jury who apparently believed that his wife enjoyed sadomasochistic sex. The jurors came to this conclusion after hearing Trish's first husband testify about their sexual history. In contrast, police reports of physical and sexual abuse by Dale's first wife were ruled inadmissible. Both Dale and Trish Crawford appeared on several television programs to discuss their experiences, and many concerned feminists in South Carolina have since campaigned to change the rape legislation (Wertheimer, 1992).

In the most recent case, John Wayne Bobbitt was charged with and acquitted of raping his wife, Lorena, in Manassas, Virginia. Lorena claimed that she had suffered years of physical and sexual abuse and that, after one incident of rape, she had severed her husband's penis with a kitchen knife. Lorena was later found innocent by reason of insanity and sentenced to a mental institution for up to 45 days to undergo evaluation (Laura X, 1994). This case and the subsequent trial received both national and international attention. The Bobbitts seemed to strike a nerve in the population, as people debated which was the more serious crime—rape or severing a penis—and how each party should be punished. Although the Bobbitt case certainly drew public attention to the problem of wife rape, the case was highly sensationalized, and the trauma that Lorena experienced was trivialized.

The notoriety of these three cases was short-lived, and wife rape has remained relatively hidden from the public eye. Indeed, the topic of wife rape receives little public attention in comparison with other issues such as date rape and domestic violence. Thus, it is not surprising that many people do not consider this to be a serious problem. The few studies that have examined the public's perception of sexual assault all reveal similar findings with regard to rape in marriage. For example, Gordon and Riger (1989) found that the majority of men and women surveyed (64% and 63% respectively) did not characterize "unwanted sexual intercourse between a husband and wife" as rape (p. 61). In a study that asked people to rank the severity of 140 crimes, "forcible rape of a former spouse" ranked 62, below selling marijuana and mugging and stealing $25 (in Finkelhor & Yllö, 1985, pp. 152-154). Clearly, the general public is unaware of the serious nature of this problem.

However, the media and the general public are not alone in neglecting the issue of wife rape and the serious ramifications of this form of sexual assault; scholars have done so as well. Diana Russell's groundbreaking book, *Rape in Marriage,* was first published in 1982;

it was based on her interviews with 87 survivors of wife rape. Also in 1982, an article on Greta Rideout appeared in *Ms.* magazine. Besides Russell's book, only one other book, *License to Rape,* by David Finkelhor and Kersti Yllö (1985) has been published on this topic in the United States. Both of these books draw on in-depth interviews with survivors of wife rape and thus are important for documenting the trauma associated with this type of violence. Furthermore, both books were instrumental in exposing the traditional tolerance of wife rape in this country and in documenting the widespread nature of this problem.

Beyond this research, wife rape has been relatively understudied compared with other forms of interpersonal violence. Some researchers have focused on its association with battering (Campbell, 1989; Frieze, 1983; Gelles, 1977; Hanneke & Shields, 1985; Walker, 1979) and the legal ramifications of the marital rape exemption statute (Augustine, 1991; Drucker, 1979; Griffin, 1980). However, compared with the amount of research devoted to other forms of violence against women and children, the attention to wife rape is conspicuously scarce. This book is an attempt to add to the available information on this subject.

The Research

In studying wife rape, I collected data from a variety of sources, which I will briefly describe. Those who want a more detailed discussion of the research process, obstacles I faced, and ethical considerations should see Appendix D.

One important source of data for this book was a survey I conducted of 1,730 service providers listed in two national directories. Of those contacted, 621 completed and returned the surveys, a response rate of about 36%. Each agency was asked about the services it offers to wife rape survivors; an analysis of the responses forms the basis of Chapter 5.

In addition, I interviewed 37 service providers about their interaction with wife rape survivors. These interviews were supplemented by my 18 months of participant observation at a rape crisis center Women Against Sexual Assault (WASA) and a battered women's shelter (Refuge).[5] As a participant observer, I attended meetings and training sessions[6] and generally observed how staff members worked with battered women and/or rape survivors. My purpose in doing this was to gain a greater sense of how workers framed the issue of wife rape and what their experiences were in interacting with survivors of wife rape on a daily basis.

The most important source of data for this book was the interviews I conducted with 40 survivors of wife rape. Their words and the experiences they shared with me constitute the core of this book.

All of the women I interviewed had been raped by their partners at least once, and all had contacted a women's agency for support. Sixty percent of the women had contacted a battered women's shelter; 23% contacted a rape crisis center; and 17% contacted both types of agencies. In this book, I define *wife rape* as any unwanted intercourse or penetration (vaginal, anal, or oral) obtained by force or threat of force or when the woman is unable to give affirmative consent (Pagelow, 1984; Russell, 1990). In this definition, I include both those women who are physically assaulted and those for whom no physical force is involved. My definition of wife rape extends beyond those legally married to include partners considered married under common law and those who have had an ongoing intimate relationship. I do this to acknowledge that one need not be legally married to suffer the trauma and consequences of being raped by one's intimate partner. Furthermore, as Campbell (1989) notes, "a marriage license probably does not change the dynamics of sexual abuse within an ongoing intimate relationship, except to make it legal in some states" (p. 336).[7] Thus, my sample includes legally married women, those who have cohabited with their partners for more than a year, and those in partnerships who share a child.[8]

It must be emphasized that my sample includes only those survivors of wife rape who sought help from a rape crisis center and/or a battered women's shelter. The majority of women sought assistance from a shelter, thus, battered women are clearly overrepresented in this sample. Furthermore, it is unclear how many survivors of wife rape identify themselves as such or seek help from rape crisis centers and/or battered women's shelters for the violence. This sample probably overrepresents those survivors of wife rape who identify as such and successfully end their violent relationships. Thus, the women in this study may not be representative of all women who are raped by their partners.

It is likely that this sample is representative of those survivors of wife rape who seek assistance from battered women's shelters and rape crisis centers. However, it is possible that those women from each agency who agreed to talk with me might be different than those who refused, in that the interviewees might have had a more positive experience with the shelter and/or rape crisis center than others. Presumably, those who left abruptly or were asked to leave the shelter because of rule violations were more likely to be dissatisfied than those who stayed for long periods of time. Those who did not find the services helpful might have been less likely to have prolonged contact (and provide updated information about addresses and phone numbers), or they may have refused to talk with me because of my affiliation with the agency.

Thus, I believe that the women I spoke with were more likely to assess the services of the agencies positively. Those women whom I was unable to reach might be those who were truly dissatisfied, and they might provide an even more negative assessment of the agencies' services.

Keeping these limitations in mind, this research is valuable for gaining a more comprehensive understanding of women's experiences of wife rape, their help-seeking behavior, and the response of service providers to this problem. The following two chapters will explore in detail how women cope with and define their experiences of sexual violence and how they seek help. This study also provides an important, in-depth look at two organizations and how they render services to this population. Chapter 4 presents two case studies that explore the response of workers at a battered women's shelter and a rape crisis center to the problem of wife rape. In the final chapter, I discuss the findings of my national survey of women's agencies and consider the policy implications of providing services to this population.

Notes

1. In this book I use the term *survivor* rather than *victim* of wife rape to indicate that these women are neither helpless nor the passive recipients of violence. Indeed, as Wiehe and Richards (1995) argue, "a survivor is one who has experienced a trauma and lives to tell about it. The term survivor implies that the victim has succeeded or endured, despite experiencing a serious trauma" (p. 5).

2. Although the sensitive nature of wife rape makes it difficult to determine the actual prevalence of this type of crime, Russell's (1990) numbers are generally considered to be valid, given that she collected information from a random sample of California residents. Other researchers (Campbell, 1989; Frieze, 1983) have used agencies, referrals, and advertisements to generate a sample of survivors of wife rape. These studies are less representative of the total population and thus not as helpful for establishing the prevalence of wife rape. However, they are valuable for providing detailed descriptions about the nature of wife rape.

3. It is important to note that wife rape is against the law in several countries, and some of these countries criminalized rape in marriage years before the United States began to address this issue. For information on wife rape in other countries, see Russell (1990) or contact Laura X at the National Clearinghouse on Marital and Date Rape. See Appendix B for the address of this organization.

4. Furthermore, in the U.S. armed forces, one can now be charged with raping one's spouse (Article 120, 1984).

5. The names of these organizations have been changed to protect the identities of workers and clients.

6. It should also be noted that I was involved in providing training programs on wife rape to employees and/or volunteers at both agencies. I began these training programs prior to my data collection at WASA and subsequent to my data collection at Refuge. The significance of these programs will be addressed later in this book.

7. According to the State Law Chart prepared by the National Clearinghouse on Marital and Date Rape (1995), the exemption from prosecution from rape is extended to unmarried cohabitors in five states—Connecticut, Delaware, Iowa, Minnesota, and West Virginia—and to dates in Delaware.

8. This definition is the same one used by the state (in which the majority of interviews were conducted) in granting individuals restraining orders against their "partners."

2

Understanding Women's Experiences of Wife Rape

The goal of this chapter is to develop a more comprehensive understanding of women's experiences of wife rape by focusing on the nature of this type of sexual violence and how women cope with it. How victims of domestic violence respond to the violence in their relationships has been studied by many researchers including Ferraro and Johnson (1983), Mills (1985), Pagelow (1992) and Walker (1979). Frieze (1983) found that women who are raped by their husbands are more likely than battered women to file legal charges and to try to leave their partners; Russell (1990) analyzed how raped wives end the violence. However, there is no research to date that systematically documents the coping strategies of wife rape survivors. As Kelly (1988) argues, women's coping strategies must be considered if we are to acknowledge the complexity of women's experiences of sexual violence and the impact of that violence on their lives. Furthermore, by exploring how women manage wife rape, we see that they "are not passive victims at the time of assault nor are [they] passive victims in relation to the consequences of abuse" (Kelly, 1988, p. 159).

To begin to explore the complexity of women's experiences of wife rape, I draw on in-depth interviews I conducted with 40 survivors of wife rape. As I explained in Chapter 1, all of these women had been raped by their partners at least once, and all had contacted a service provider for assistance at some point.

The Sample

There was considerable variation by race, age, and socioeconomic status among the women I interviewed. With regard to race, 60% of the participants were white, 22% were African American, and 18% were Latina. The age of women in this study ranged from 18 to 61, with a median age of 37. The length of time women in this sample had been with their partners varied from 1 to 36 years.

The majority of women in this study (58%) would be characterized as middle class (based on income, education, and occupation), and 40% were lower class. Upper-class women (there was one in this sample) were highly underrepresented in this sample, which is not surprising given that upper-class women are less likely to use battered women's shelters.

About one third of the women in this sample had attended college or had a college degree, and 10% were either attending graduate school or held graduate degrees. About 28% were employed in white-collar or professional occupations, and 25% were in blue-collar occupations. Women who were unemployed (47%) are overrepresented in this sample. Again, this most likely reflects the fact that many of the women were interviewed while staying at a battered women's shelter and had been forced to give up their jobs to relocate. The importance of this demographic data will be discussed in later chapters. For now, let us turn to a central question of this book, how do women experience wife rape?

Women's Experiences of Wife Rape

Within the larger society, wife rape is often understood as a relatively innocuous incident in which a husband wants to have sex, his wife rejects him, and he holds her down on the bed and has intercourse with her. Although a few of the women in this sample experienced this type of sexual assault, this scenario was far from the

Table 2.1 Type of Wife Rape

Type	Number of Women	Percentage (n = 40)
Force-only	10	25
Battering	13	33
Sadistic	2	5
Combination force-only and battering	8	20
Combination battering and sadistic	7	17

norm. Indeed, the women I interviewed described a wide range of experiences, from assaults that were relatively quick in duration and involved little physical force to sadistic, torturous episodes that lasted for hours.

Based on their interviews with 50 women, Finkelhor and Yllö (1985) identified three types of wife rape. Incidents in which women were not battered but experienced "only as much force as necessary to coerce their wives into sex" (p. 38) were characterized as *force-only rapes. Battering rapes* were identified as "forced sex combined with beatings" (p. 37) and accounted for the largest number of cases. The third category, which applied to about half a dozen women in their sample and largely involved men who used pornography, was defined as *obsessive rapes.* Finkelhor and Yllö characterized obsessive rapes as those incidents in which physical force was combined with "the strange and the perverse" (p. 50). This category closely resembles what Nicholas Groth (1979) calls *sadistic rapes,* in which assaults typically involve bondage and torture. In this study I too will refer to these rapes as sadistic rapes.

Like Russell (1990) and Finkelhor and Yllö (1985), I suspect that there are many other types of wife rape. Furthermore, the type of violence women experienced often changed over the course of the relationship. However, these classifications reflect how women themselves talked about their experiences of sexual violence—from being coerced to have sex when they really didn't want to, to being terrorized with sadistic acts involving torture. Thus, I find Finkelhor and Yllö's categorizations useful for beginning to discuss the nature of the violence these women faced. Table 2.1 describes the types of sexual violence experienced by the women in this sample.

Force-Only Rape

In my study, 10 of the women described force-only rapes.[1] Although they were all physically battered at other times during their relationship, the sexual abuse was generally not characterized by physical violence. For example, Abigail told me,

> He shoved me down on the bed very forcefully, and I said, "What are you doing? . . . No, I don't want this." And there [were] no preliminaries and no tenderness. Nothing. And he entered me and it was painful and I just remember being so repulsed.

Kayla remembered this incident:

> He gave me that wild look. You know, that sick look. And I thought, "Oh no, I don't want to do this." But I just knew there was no way to pass it off or get away. . . . I didn't want to, but I felt pinned down and forced by his weight on top of me. I just wanted to get it over with.

The women in the force-only category described incidents of sexual abuse devoid of excessive physical violence. However, they talked about their fear of physical violence if they resisted their partners' sexual advances. As Cory told me, "If I resisted, he would beat me up, so I learned not to resist and I just gave in." Lisa said,

> I always gave in. He never forced me; he just expected it every weekend, and I just did it to keep the peace. I just did it to get it over with so he would go to sleep and leave me alone. Then I wouldn't have to put up with him yelling at the kids and yelling at me.

When I asked Lisa what might have happened if she had resisted her partner, she said she didn't know: "I never wanted to find out, so I just gave in." Lisa's partner had a long history of extreme physical violence, which included giving her numerous black eyes and a broken nose; she was quite frightened of him.

Several other women in this force-only category experienced severe physical violence at other times during their relationship, and their fear of the physical repercussions is what motivated many of them not to resist their partners' sexual advances. However, it is significant to note that these women were not freely consenting to have intercourse; they only acquiesced out of fear that physical violence would occur if they did not. Other women, although not freely choosing to have sex, did so out of a sense of obligation. Kayla said, "I thought I had to. Nobody ever told me I had the right to say no. I knew it was yucky and I dreaded it, but I thought I had to do it." Paula described her reasons:

> He always wanted to have sex. He was jealous, and if he didn't have sex with me every single day, that meant that I was with another guy and that was his theory. From the time I was 18, I had sex every single day for the first year we were married, and maybe I had 2 days off when I had my period. But we did it every day because he wanted to and I thought I had to.

Supporting findings by Finkelhor and Yllö (1985), these women were no less upset or humiliated than other wife rape survivors, simply because these incidents were devoid of excess force. Indeed, Lisa told me that after each rape, "I was real upset and I would cry afterwards. I felt so terrible and it didn't even bother him. He didn't care." Noelle, who had been raped by an acquaintance when she was a teenager, was particularly traumatized by her husband's attack. She said,

> That's [rape] the worst thing he could have done knowing my background and knowing how I felt about the issue—it's a violation of trust and commitment and the whole bit and compound it with knowing my background, and it was the worst thing he could have done to me.

Thus, we see that the women in this sample who experienced force-only rape suffered serious emotional consequences from being raped by their partners even though they did not suffer from excessive physical violence.

Battering Rape

All of the women in this sample experienced physical violence at some point during their relationships, and several were severely battered by their partners. Again, this is probably the result of my sample, which was drawn largely from a battered women's shelter. Russell (1990) argues that not all women who are raped by their partners are battered wives. However, researchers such as Browne (1993), Campbell (1989), and Shields and Hanneke (1983) have noted that wife rape is more likely to occur in marriages characterized by extreme physical violence.

In this study, women who had been severely battered talked about common injuries, such as black eyes, broken bones, blood clots in their heads, and knife wounds. In a particularly violent incident, Nina described how her partner (who was angered by her pregnancy) dragged her into the woods, where he beat and raped her and then used a knife to slice open her abdomen. While not all of the women in my sample were subjected to such extreme forms of physical violence, about 70% of them experienced battering rapes at some point.

For some, the physical violence regularly accompanied the sexual abuse. For example, Barbara told me,

> He would fight me and then he would always rip all of my clothes off me. I don't have hardly any clothes left because he always ripped off my clothes, and I was naked. Then he would try to lay on me and put it in. Sometimes I was able to fight him off, and I would fight like wild, and he wouldn't be able to get it in. But usually he would [succeed in penetrating her], and he put me in the hospital a lot. He broke my nose and my jaw and cut my wrists.

Karen remembered a typically violent incident:

> I was cooking, and he came out and started to hassle me, and I burned the eggs and then he started beating me because I had burned them. So he beat me up for a half hour, I guess, and then he said, "OK, bitch, get back upstairs," and I knew he wanted sex just by the way he said it. I said, "I can't do that now because I'm really upset and I can't make love to someone who beat me up" . . . and he said "now," and he turned off the stove and ripped off my pajamas and started punching me . . . and I got into the corner and was all curled up and he picked me up and threw me on the bed and did his thing. It was disgusting, and afterward I got up and threw up.

For many women, like Karen, the rape followed on the heels of the physical abuse when their partners were attempting to reconcile. For example, Jen said, "He sexually assaulted me a couple of times and always after he beat me up. He would want sex, and he would actually think in his own mind that he really hadn't done anything." Melissa told me,

He would beat me and then take it. He would choke me. He put his elbow in my throat and choked me. He would throw anything he could get his hands on—ashtrays, or whatever, he broke my fingers and hands. He was real violent. He threw knives at me, and he would throw me naked into the street and pour cold water on me and make me stay out there in the winter . . . then he would make me have sex and then go and eat a sandwich. I never understood how he could do that. How can you do that to somebody?

Pam described having similar feelings when her partner beat and then raped her: "The worst part was after he would beat me, you know, and then he wanted to sleep with me and say 'I'm sorry.' . . . I couldn't understand that, how can you do that after you beat somebody up that bad?"

Other women in this sample experienced battering rapes frequently, but not necessarily all the time. For example, Sonya experienced both force-only rapes and battering rapes at various times in her relationship. She said,

Sometimes we would go to bed, and he would push my legs aside and force sex on me. Or he would grab my head and force me [to give him oral sex]. . . . Other times he would beat the crap out of me in bed or hold a gun to my head to force me.

Usually Debbie was battered and raped at the same time. However, on several occasions, her husband sadistically tortured her with objects as well. She told me: "To say he was very rough is an understatement. He beat me until I was bruised and bleeding and then used anything—like a hairbrush, broken beer bottle, or anything—to put inside me." Like 37% of the women in this sample, Debbie saw the nature of the violence change over the course of the relationship. Most frequently, the pattern was from force-only rapes to increasingly violent, battering rapes. However, like Debbie, several women experienced battering rapes that sometimes escalated into sadistic assaults.

Sadistic Rape

The third type of wife rape, sadistic rape, was experienced by a total of nine of the women in this sample at some point in their relationships. These women characterized their experiences not only as physically violent but also as involving "perverse" acts or torture. Seven women experienced both battering rapes and sadistic rapes. However, two were always sadistically raped—for both this occurred more than 20 times during the course of their relationships. For example, Tanya was regularly choked to the point of passing out and then raped by her partner. She told me,

> He was really into watching porno movies, and he tried to make me do all sorts of things. And I [didn't] like it. He hurt my stomach so bad because I was pregnant, and he was making me do these things. I think he's a sadist—he pulls my hair and punches me and slaps me and makes me pass out.

One third of the women in this sample mentioned that their partners used pornographic material and frequently forced them to enact what they had seen. After viewing pornography, two women were forced to have intercourse with other people while their husbands watched. The use of pornography was clearly associated with the most sadistic rapists.[2]

For several of the women in this study, bondage was a usual occurrence in their experiences of sexual violence. Lorraine, who was regularly sadistically raped, remembered

> just waking up and being tied to the bed by my arms and legs, and the thing that woke me up was him touching me [vaginally] with a feather and me waking up in shock. And he had this thing about taking pictures of it all and trying to open me up [vaginally]. So he would use his fist and other objects and then make me do exercises on the toilet to tighten [my vagina] up again.

The women who described sadistic incidents of sexual assault suffered particularly severe physical and emotional trauma as a result of the violence. This is likely the result of both the terroristic nature of the assaults they experienced and the great frequency with which they were raped by their partners.

Frequency of Wife Rape

The experiences of women who were raped by their partners differed not only by the type of violence they suffered but also in terms of the frequency of the incidents. For a few women in this sample,

Table 2.2 Frequency of Wife Rape

Frequency	Number of Women	Percentage (n = 40)
Once	7	17
Twice	3	8
3-10 times	6	15
11-20 times	2	5
20 times or more	22	55

rape was a relatively rare occurrence. For example, Abigail was married to her partner for 25 years and was raped once early in the relationship. Other women were raped so frequently they lost count. Debbie was raped as often as three times a day over a period of 8 years. We see from Table 2.2 that most women (55%) were raped frequently—more than 20 times during the course of their relationships. Finkelhor and Yllö (1985) also found that 50% of the women in their sample were raped more than 20 times. Although there is a wide range of experiences represented in this sample, rape was not an infrequent occurrence but the norm for most women.

Types of Forced Sexual Behavior

Women who are raped by their husbands experience not only vaginal penetration but a variety of unwanted, forced sexual acts. In fact, Peacock (1995) writes that marital rape survivors are more likely to experience unwanted oral and anal intercourse than women who are raped by acquaintances. About 57% of the women in my sample were vaginally raped by their partners. However, 40% of the women reported at least one incident of anal rape, and 33% had been forced to perform oral sex on their partners.[3] Thus, we see considerable variation in the type of sexual violence women experienced and the frequency with which they were raped by their partners.

Causes of Wife Rape

The women in this sample offered many explanations for the rapes inflicted on them by their partners. However, it is significant to note that these explanations were offered after they had ended the violence.

While the relationships were ongoing, many of the women said, they blamed themselves for the violence. In retrospect, they were more likely to hold their husbands responsible for sexually abusing them.

Entitlement to Sex

One of the most popular explanations women offered was that their partner believed that he had the right to sexual intercourse on demand; when refused, he had the right to take it. Such thinking is created and perpetuated by the traditional patriarchal family structure defined by men's domination and women's subordination. As Finkelhor and Yllö (1985) note, the ideal of sex as a conjugal right is particularly evident among men who rape their wives. Their research reveals that many men feel a sense of entitlement to their wives' bodies and thus do not regard forced sex as rape.[4]

The majority of women in this sample indicated that their husbands felt a sense of ownership that gave them the sexual rights to their wives' bodies at all times. For example, Wanda remembered that her husband told her repeatedly, "That's my body—my ass, my tits, my body. You gave that to me when you married me and that belongs to me." Similarly, Emily recalled that on the night her husband raped her, "he was saying something like I'm his wife and I'm supposed to have sex with him and by law I was his or something like that—his possession."

When several of the women in this study informed their partners that the act they had committed was rape, the men still adamantly denied this because of their sense of sexual entitlement. For example, Rhonda's husband told her, "You're my wife—this ain't rape." When Terri confronted her partner, he said, "Girl, I didn't rape you. How can I rape my own woman?" Even after eight of the women in this sample filed criminal charges against their partners for sexual assault, the majority of the men continued to deny that their actions could legally be rape. Pam told me,

> I remember one time he [her husband] told the judge, "That's my wife, you can't tell me what to do with her." The judge said, "Oh really. I'm gonna give you time to think about it in jail." . . . He [her husband] thought he could do anything—cut me, beat me, have sex with me, because [he said] you're my wife and I'm your husband.

Several women in this study said that when they were forbidden, for medical reasons, to have sex with their partners, their risk of being raped increased because their partners' sense of entitlement was challenged. In one of the most brutal examples in my study, Stacey returned home from having a cesarean section to have this encounter with her husband, who was a physician:

> I told him [my husband] I couldn't have intercourse, and he told me "Skin heals in 72 hours." I'll never forget that. Then he kneeled with a knee on either side of my shoulders and smacked his penis across my face and said, "You suck me, bitch."

Stacey's husband reasserted "his rights" by forcing her to have oral intercourse, after which he sodomized her.

This sense of entitlement often lasts even after the couple is separated or divorced, as was the case with 20% of the women in this sample. For example, after she was separated, Lisa was raped frequently by her partner when he showed up to give her his child support payments. She said, "I dreaded the weekends. It was like clockwork, and he would just make me do it, and I knew it was coming and that made it worse."

As the research of Finkelhor and Yllö (1985), Frieze (1983), and Russell (1990) reveals, women are particularly at risk of being raped when they are separated or divorced, because despite the dissolution of the marital bond, this sense of entitlement and the belief that their (ex) wives are their property live on.

Rape as Punishment

Several of the women in my sample believed that the sexual abuse was their partners' attempt to punish either their loved ones or the women themselves. For example, Sally recalled the following exchange that occurred one night, just before her husband raped her:

> I think he thought that I was his wife, and he could do anything to me, and if he wanted sex, he got sex. And he could do anything and do no wrong and I belonged to him. Like one night when my daughter came back from her date, he flipped because the boy didn't shake his hand, and he screamed, "She's never going out with him again." And he went on and on and said, "Now it's time for you to pay. It's time to pay up like you did the other night."

Sally was punished for the actions of her daughter's boyfriend. Other women were raped as punishment for their own "sins," as Natalie described here:

> A lot of times it [rape] happened because he was so jealous. He always thought that I was looking at other men. Like the time my brother and his friend—who I grew up with—were over, and he thought I was looking at his friend, and he was really mad. He started hitting me and then forced me to have sex.

Tanya remembered a similar linkage between punishment and rape:

> He [her partner] would try to choke me, and then I would pass out. Then he would rape me. He would put me to sleep and then rape me. Sometimes when we were out somewhere, and he didn't like something I did, he would say "You wanna go to sleep?" and laugh like it was real funny. It was like a punishment.

Like Natalie and Tanya, several women in this study recalled that their partners forced them "to pay" sexually as punishment. Ultimately, these women perceived the assaults as their partners' attempt to control their behavior.

Rape as a Form of Control

The majority of women in this sample saw the sexual violence as their partners' way to assert power and control over them. As Pam told me,

> The more control he thought he was losing, the worse it got. If I got a job or I was doing good, he would take it away. He would beat me up and force me [to have sex] just to get that control back.

Similarly, Lorraine recalled that her husband "had this real need to control me. To be master over me and he tried to do different things sexually with me to control me. Like putting his fist inside of me to open me up."

Nine of the women told me that their partners, in an ultimate attempt at control, raped them in order to impregnate them so that they would not leave the relationship. In five cases, their partners' efforts were successful. For example, Annabel said, "We had five children. I think he raped me to keep me pregnant all the time because he knew I would never leave the kids."

Whereas some partners used pregnancy to control their wives, several women told me that their husbands were angered by their pregnancies, possibly because this represented a loss of control over them. Indeed, three women in this study talked about their partners' attempts to make them "lose the baby" through increased violence and/or coerced abortions because they believed that their wives had been unfaithful to them. For example, Wanda recalled that her husband

> tried to force me to have an abortion because he didn't believe it was his child. . . . When I refused to get an abortion, he took me to [the] women's clinic, and I was on the table and I was far enough along that the doctor said he couldn't do it.

Although he was not successful in forcing his wife to have an abortion, her husband continued to sexually and physically abuse her throughout her pregnancy, Wanda said, possibly with the hope that she would lose the baby.

In this sample, pregnancy was a factor that appeared to place women at a higher risk of being both physically and sexually abused. Researchers such as Browne (1992), Campbell, Poland, Waller, and Ager (1992), and Gelles (1988) have noted the correlation between battering and pregnancy. Campbell (1989) found that women who were sexually abused by their partners were also more likely to be abused during pregnancy. One third of the women in my sample spoke about the increase in physical and sexual violence they experienced during pregnancy. Several women said the sexual abuse happened for the first time while they were pregnant:

> The sexual stuff started when I got pregnant. (Tanya)

> It started right before the baby was born. When I was pregnant, the doctor said not to have relations, but he kept wanting it. I had hard pregnancies. (Delilah)

> It happened for the first time when I was 4 months pregnant, and I was scared for the baby. (Danielle)

The women who were raped during their pregnancies were traumatized, not only by the sexual assaults but also by the fear of how their unborn children might be affected by their partners' violent behavior. However, most of the women felt that there was little they could do to stop the sexual abuse and their husbands' attempts to dominate them in this way.

In conclusion, we see that there are a variety of explanations offered by women to explain the sexual violence in their lives. Furthermore, it is clear that the sexual violence the women in this sample experienced varied greatly. Indeed, no stereotypical depiction of the "average wife rape" emerges from their descriptions.

Despite individual differences among the participants' experiences, there were similarities in how these women managed the sexual violence. Let us now turn to a central question of this book: How do women cope with their experiences of wife rape?

Coping With Wife Rape

Trudy Mills's (1985) research on battered women reveals that women implement a variety of coping strategies to deal with the violence in their lives and protect themselves from harm. Mills (1995) argues that women who are abused by their husbands must manage the violence and that this involves

> the attachment of meaning to the violence and the development of strategies to cope with it. The meanings the woman attaches to the violence and the resources she believes she has shape strategies for living with, or ending, the violence. (p. 107)

In her analysis of the impact of sexual violence on the lives of women, Liz Kelly (1988) explores how women cope with sexual violence. She defines coping as

> the actions taken to avoid or control distress. Women's coping responses are active, constructive adaptions to the experiences of abuse. The responses of any particular woman will depend on how she defines her experience, the context within which it occurs, and the resources which are available to her at the time and subsequently. (p. 160)

Just as battered women and other survivors of repeated acts of violence learn to manage the violence, my research indicates that wife rape survivors too develop strategies to cope with their experiences of sexual abuse, beginning with the first incident.[5]

The First Incident

For the majority of women in this study, the first forced sexual experience was merely one in a long line of abuses to come. Indeed, only seven women were able to escape the relationship after having been raped only once. Six of these women terminated their relationships immediately after the first incident of rape.[5] Those women were either separated or seriously considering separation from their partners at the time of the rape, and several had the economic resources to survive on their own. For example, Rhonda and her husband were separated at the time of the incident but maintained an amicable relationship. On the night of the rape, he entered her house, which was not unusual, and then, she says, "It was like something just snapped in him. He grabbed me and said, 'We gonna have sex, I need to fuck.' " Rhonda was raped for 7 hours before her husband finally left. At the time of the rape, Rhonda owned her own home, had a job, and was already separated from her assailant, so the decision to remove herself from any further contact with her husband was easy to make.

Whereas Rhonda's circumstances allowed her to immediately end all contact with her husband, most of the women in this study were not in a position to do this. For example, although Karen also identified her first experience as rape, it took her 2 months to save money and finalize her plans to leave. She was raped 11 more times during this period.

As Russell (1990) argues, economic factors are extremely important in understanding why women leave or remain with the men who rape them. Given the large number of women who were unemployed in my sample and the small number of those who immediately left the violent relationship, it is difficult to conclusively determine the relationship between occupation and likelihood of ending the violence. However, in my sample, those women who were employed were more likely to end the violence quickly by leaving their partners. Those who were unemployed, particularly women with children, were less likely to leave immediately.

The vast majority of women in this sample did not leave the relationship after the first incident but instead tried to manage the violence. After the first incident, all of the women reported feeling a similar sense of shock that the assault was happening to them and a general feeling of disbelief that someone they loved was responsible for their pain. Debbie is typical in her response to the first rape:

> The first time, I thought, "I don't believe this is happening, I just don't believe it." I was in shock—totally numb—and I don't know how I ever got over being that numb. It just blew me out, and I thought this can't be happening to me.

Most of the women reported that they thought the first assault was an aberrant incident that would never happen again. Frieze and Bulman (1983) report that shock, confusion, anxiety, fear, helplessness, and a belief that this will only happen once are common psychological responses to victimization. Indeed, for most victims of haphazard crimes, this coping mechanism of treating the incident as a single occurrence may suffice. However, many survivors of wife rape (more than 80% of women in this sample) learn that the first incident is not aberrant but an ongoing problem. Thus, after the initial shock has ceased, survivors of wife rape are forced either to develop strategies to manage the violence or end the relationship.

Managing the Violence

Mills (1985) argues that the two fundamental goals in managing violence are protecting oneself from injury and justifying the continuation of the relationship. During the course of the relationship, a woman's coping strategies often change as it becomes clear to her that she will or will not be able to avoid an assault. My interviews revealed that a variety of strategies were employed by women to protect themselves, including minimizing the risk of violence, diminishing injuries once the violence had begun, and emotionally surviving the violence.

Minimizing the Risk of Violence

A primary way women in this sample tried to cope with being raped by their partners was to minimize the risk that violence would occur. As Sally told me,

You know what's gonna happen, and you're trying to think in your brain, how can I stop this without getting hurt? And you don't know how to stop it without angering him because you know you're going to get killed, and it's like looking a murderer straight in the eye, and they have this cold-blooded look, and you know you're dead unless you can do something.

There were several strategies implemented by women to minimize the risk that they would be sexually assaulted.

Active Resistance

Most women in this sample attempted, on at least one occasion, to minimize the risk of violence by physically resisting their partners. Like the women in Finkelhor and Yllö's (1985) study, one quarter of the women in this sample were successful at least once in resisting their husbands' attempts to rape them. For example, Erica physically resisted to the point where her husband grew tired and gave up. On one occasion, Samantha was able to kick her husband in the groin and escape. Several other women used weapons, such as guns or knives, to deter their partners; Terri stabbed her partner in the arm with a kitchen knife. In one particularly dramatic account, Sally was able to get away from her husband:

I don't know what happened. For some reason I was stronger [that day], and I don't know what it was but I actually fought back. When he started holding my hands and pushing me down and forcing off my clothes—with all my might, I took my knee and rammed it between his legs. And when I did that, he was weak and I saw I had that power—that strength. I could do it.

Sally's strength incapacitated her husband and gave her enough time to get to her car. When her husband jumped onto the hood of the car, she drove him directly to the police station and honked her horn until the police came outside and arrested him. Clearly these women were courageous and creative in their attempts to resist their partners' attacks. However, most of the women in this sample said they learned not to resist but merely to "give in." Debbie recalled how she quickly learned not to resist her husband:

I live in an apartment where you go up the steps to get in, and do you know how many times I've been dragged up the stairs? Get away? It just doesn't happen. So I learned quick, and then I never fought back or anything because it would just prolong the agony. It's over quicker if I just give in.

Kayla described a similar incident: "I knew the boundaries, and I knew not to push his buttons. I knew if I went beyond the boundaries, I would be hurt. So it was safer for me sometimes to just do it [have sex with him]." This nonresistance should not be construed as women freely deciding to have sex. The majority of women in this study defined the cases when they did not physically resist as forced sex or rape because they were not acts to which they had freely consented. Indeed, their nonresistance indicates reasonable behavior on the part of these women, who were trying desperately to minimize their injuries.

Avoidance

Most of the women in this sample found that a more successful strategy than active resistance was simple avoidance. Indeed, several women tried a tactic similar to Natalie's: "He would come home from work angry over something and take it out on me. So I would try to stay out of his way." Danielle knew that she was particularly at risk for being sexually assaulted after her husband watched pornographic movies, so she made extra efforts to avoid him at these times.

Many women avoided the bedroom, feigned sleep, or went to bed only after they were certain their partners were asleep. For example, Kayla recalled,

I kept busy. I went to school and to work and to the gym and I walked 4 miles every night. I was physically and emotionally exhausted and I would fall asleep downstairs with the TV at night because I didn't want to go upstairs to bed.

Other women in this sample used more direct tactics to avoid their husbands. For example, Debbie particularly feared her husband when he had been drinking. When he came home drunk, she regularly took advantage of his ulcer by putting tabasco sauce into his food. The result was that he became very thirsty and continued to drink more beer, not realizing why he was so thirsty. Debbie says that "if I was lucky, he would pass out and leave me alone." Otherwise, Debbie was forced to have sexual intercourse until he passed out from sheer exhaustion.

Placating Their Husbands

The most popular tactic for minimizing the risk of assault was for women to placate their husbands. Placation took many forms, including not seeing close friends of whom their husbands did not approve, quitting jobs, distancing themselves from their families, maintaining a clean home, having dinner ready at specific times, and keeping the children quiet at all times. These were all components of what these women perceived as their role as "good wives," and they tried actively to meet their husbands' expectations in order to avoid violent episodes. The majority of women told stories similar to this account by Annabel, who remained with her husband for 29 years: "I felt if I could just be what he wanted—a good wife—and stay at home, then he would stop." Cory remembered thinking, "OK, I can play housewife, I can do that."

Like many battered women, most of the women in this sample understood that if they could fulfill their partners' expectations about being a good wife and mother, they would reduce their risk of experiencing violence. However, it should be emphasized that these women were not merely passive in their acceptance of their husbands' demands and gender role expectations; placating their partners was an active coping strategy used to minimize their risk of being abused (Kelly, 1988).

Minimizing Injuries Once the Violence Had Begun

Although most of the women went to great lengths to please their husbands, they all learned that they could not manipulate every situation and avoid being sexually assaulted. Thus, they tried to minimize their injuries as a way of maintaining some form of control over the violence. Stacey said, "I would try to manipulate him during the sex, not for my own needs or orgasms, but to control his anger and try to reduce it so I wouldn't get really hurt." Many of the women tried to appease their husbands sexually in order to minimize their risk of harm. For example, Annabel knew that she had to "service him [her husband] to keep the peace." Natalie told me, "I would fake it (orgasm)—I was the best damn actress—I could have won an award. I even did things to him when there were tears in my eyes."

One quarter of the women in this sample said they sometimes performed oral sex on their husbands, although they despised this act, so that the abuse would end quickly. This was particularly difficult for several of the women, who were incest survivors and recalled being forced to engage in fellatio with their assailants when they were children.

Other women in this sample recalled engaging in what they referred to as "perverse" activities, such as anal intercourse and bondage, to reduce their risk of injury. Although she despised having anal intercourse, Lorraine remembered that she allowed her husband to do this so that he would not severely batter her in front of their children. Similarly, Debbie remembered how she would lay quietly while he "stuck everything from a hairbrush to his gun in my vagina" because she feared the internal damage that might be caused if she struggled. Thus, we see that through a variety of means women tried to minimize their risk of being assaulted and the physical harm that they suffered at the hands of their husbands.

Emotionally Surviving Wife Rape

When rape appeared inevitable, these women had little choice but to focus their energy on limiting their injury and emotionally surviving the attack. All of the women who experienced more than one assault described mechanisms that allowed them to survive the actual rape. As Judith Herman (1981) found in her work with incest survivors, many victims of sexual assault resort to psychological measures to minimize the trauma. Some women find their time perception and sensory perception altered as they disassociate themselves from the experience or treat it as if it is happening to somebody else (Hawkins, 1991). Kelly (1988) defines this process of "cutting off" as not just a coping strategy but also an act of resistance. In doing this, a woman refuses to let her partner control her mind and feelings.

One of the most prevalent survival strategies was best described by Debbie as "orbing out." She recalled,

He would be all over me, and then I just went out in my mind—I just wasn't there anymore. I took myself somewhere else, and I found out later that I had done that a lot. Even growing up and all, if anything hurts me, I orb out—I get totally numb.

Cory, another survivor of incest, told of a similar strategy: "I learned early on to separate myself from what's going on, and I wouldn't think about anything when it [wife rape] happened."

Several of the women in this sample said that they had blocked out so much, their sense of time had been altered. Debbie recalled,

> I think that's [orbing out] how I got through it. I just didn't deal, this went on for a total of 8 years, and I don't think anyone could deal with all that [abuse]. I know there are things I don't remember, and there are blanks, and as far as time sequence goes, I can't put those 8 years in order. As much as I've tried, I've looked at pictures and I can't order them.

Jen also remembered that she "blocked out so much. Days would go by [when] I have no clue what happened."

Although this strategy was consistently employed, particularly by the one quarter of the women in this study who were survivors of incest, some women reported out-of-body experiences only during certain episodes. For example, Karen described having "out-of-body experiences—like I was watching from a corner of the room because I couldn't feel anything"—only during the sexual assaults but not during the physical assaults. Similarly, Annabel described having an out-of-body experience only during the most severe rape. She said, "I just focused from somewhere above on my arm, which he had twisted under me like [I was] a rag doll. I didn't see the sex as happening to me. It was happening to someone else with a twisted arm."

Several other women said they coped with the actual rape by focusing their thoughts ironically on the happy days of their marriages or on other aspects of their lives. For example, Kayla recalled, "I would lay there and pretend it's not happening to me. I would think of shopping or the kids or whatever else I had to do." Others, such as Rebecca and Wanda, repeated the same phrase continually in their minds in order to distract themselves from what was happening and help them to cope with the assaults.

All of these mechanisms enabled the survivors to cope during the actual time of crisis and to minimize emotional trauma.

Emotional Survival After Wife Rape

My interviews with wife rape survivors revealed that women not only developed strategies for coping during the actual sexual assaults, but they also developed strategies for emotional survival after each incident of sexual abuse. Kelly (1988) defines emotional survival as "the extent to which women are able to reconstruct their lives so that the experience of sexual violence does not have an overwhelming and continuing negative impact on their lives" (p. 163).

Following their experiences of wife rape, the women in this sample, like other sexual assault survivors, worked not only to exist but also to put back together the pieces of their lives. Six women in this study began to do this by terminating their relationships with their partners immediately following their first experience of wife rape. Thus, as I indicated earlier, they did not take steps to manage the violence. They emotionally survived the assault by distancing themselves from their partners, seeking the help of service providers (as I will detail in the following chapters), and turning to friends.

Gwenn was raped once by her partner after she returned home from having major surgery. Following the rape, she remembered getting dressed and leaving the house in a daze:

> I wound up at the police department, and then I found out husbands can rape their wives, so they sent me to a doctor for a rape test [kit] and then . . . I signed a criminal complaint and called [a rape crisis center] the next day.

Emily took an equally active approach after her husband raped her:

> I made a big stink after it. I made him get out. I was throwing his furniture and things out the window, and I didn't give a you-know-what who heard it. I was cursing and hollering the whole time. . . . Then I talked to my mother about what happened.

However, the majority of women in this sample were raped multiple times by their partners. These women developed strategies to cope after each assault. Kayla typifies the reaction of many women in this sample. She recalled what happened one time after she was raped:

> He fell asleep and I got up and cleaned myself up and then I pretended that nothing happened. I thought about the kids coming over, and

> I just didn't deal with it [the rape]. I thought to myself, it wasn't that bad.

Kayla's recollection reveals the complex process of coping after sexual abuse and indicates several of the strategies women I interviewed used to put their lives back together again—cleaning themselves up, forgetting about the incident, justifying the assault, and minimizing the effects of the violence.

Like other survivors of sexual assault, most of the women I interviewed felt the need to "be clean" following their experiences of rape. For example, Sally told me,

> I went into the shower and I washed myself and scrubbed myself. I did everything a rape victim would do. Everything. It was like you knew what had been done to you and that this was something all rape victims do. And you knew you had to heal yourself because if you didn't heal yourself, nobody else would.

After each sexual assault, Sara said she would "take shower after shower because I felt so dirty and I couldn't get clean."

In addition to bathing, the majority of women in this sample talked of their attempts to forget about the sexual abuse. Lisa recalled, "I would always leave the room afterwards. I would go and watch TV and try to forget it. I couldn't stay in the room, and it helped to leave and try to forget." Delilah said that after every incident she "just wanted to forget about it and hope the next time isn't too soon. I would try to make excuses for not going to bed with this person and try to forget." Others said they "tried to block it out," or they "just wouldn't think about" the sexual abuse.

Two other strategies women used were to rationalize the violence and minimize the severity of the assault. As Russell (1990) notes, it is important for women who decide to stay in the relationship, either because they do not want to leave or are unable to leave the marriage, to discount the trauma of the rape. Similarly, Kelly (1988) notes that minimizing the effects of sexual violence allows women to define the violence in a way in which they do not have to immediately act, possibly because they see no other available options or because they fear the consequences of their actions. Thus, for most women to be able to remain in the marriage, they must "work" on their emotions, transforming the social reality of their situation, so that they do not see themselves as victims or their husbands as rapists.

Rationalizing the Violence

Many abused wives reconstruct their experiences by holding themselves, rather than their husbands, responsible (Ferraro & Johnson, 1983; Mills, 1985). Although self-blame is a characteristic more commonly associated with wives who are battered than with those who are raped, a significant number of raped wives (estimates range from 6% to 20%) engage in self-blame (Finkelhor & Yllö, 1985; Frieze, 1983; Russell, 1990). Studies by Finkelhor and Yllö (1985) and Frieze (1983) indicate that the length of time a woman remains in the violent relationship and the extent to which she holds traditional ideals about the family are directly related to self-blame.

In this sample, one third of the women initially blamed themselves to some extent for their husbands' actions. Many of these women felt they had failed in their roles as wives so they were able to rationalize that it was their own fault that the forced sex occurred. For example, both Sonya and Cory were incest survivors who were generally not interested in having sexual intercourse with their partners. They felt their unresponsiveness was the cause of the sexual abuse. Sonya said,

> I wouldn't let him touch me for the first 2 months after we got married because of what I went through with my father . . . and I was afraid he was going to go and get an annulment, and I feel like part of the problem of our marriage is because I can't. It's like I want to have sex with him, but I keep having flashbacks about what happened to me, and I just can't handle it. And I know he's my husband.

These women viewed sex as their marital obligation and felt their husbands were being neglected because they were unable to fulfill their duties. Thus, they did not, at least initially, blame their husbands for raping them.

Three other women I interviewed did not blame their husbands for assaulting them but instead blamed drug or alcohol use for triggering the attacks. Crack cocaine was one substance that several women blamed for changing their partners from loving individuals into sexually and physically abusive men.[6] Terri remembered the change:

> When we got together, everything was great, and then after a couple of years, he started using drugs . . . and he turned into a totally different person and he's like a transformer. The drugs do that to him. .

These examples indicate that rather than viewing their husbands as assailants, these women perceived them as the victims in some way. By constructing the violence in this way, their husbands were free from blame, and they were able to remain in their relationships and cope with the sexual abuse.

Minimizing the Severity of the Violence

In her research, Kelly (1990) found that it was not uncommon for victims of rape to minimize or "limit the impact of incidents that they defined as abusive to some degree" (p. 126). Many of the women in this sample also minimized the extent of the sexual violence they had suffered. For example, after each rape, Debbie would tell herself, "That wasn't that bad. I got through that one so I'll get through another." Similarly, Becky thought, "I love him and I know he really loves me, so it [the abuse] wasn't so bad."

These women were hesitant to acknowledge the severity of their experiences because for a variety of reasons, including emotional and economic ties, they were not in a position to leave. Thus, rather than leave the relationship, they redefined their experiences in ways that were acceptable to them and developed elaborate coping strategies allowing them to survive from day to day. However, eventually all of these women reached a point where they were unable to cope with the violence any longer and ended their relationships.

Summary

In this chapter, we focused on the nature of wife rape and saw that women's experiences vary greatly, not only in terms of frequency, but also with regard to the types of sexual assault they are forced to endure. We also saw that women tried to manage the violence in their lives in a variety of ways. Some immediately ended their relationships, whereas others tried to minimize their risk of being raped and focused their energies on emotionally surviving each attack because they felt unable to leave. It is important to emphasize that, regardless of the coping mechanisms the women in this sample used, all of them eventually chose to leave their partners in order to end the violence. In the next chapter, we explore the complex process by which women define their experiences as rape. This is intrinsically tied to how they end the violence.

Notes

1. Finkelhor and Yllö (1985) found that 40% of their sample experienced force-only rapes. The relatively low number of force-only rapes in my study likely reflects the fact that the sample was largely drawn from women who contacted battered women's shelters; these women may have been more likely to have experienced physical violence.

2. For more information on the correlation between sexual abuse and pornography, see Russell (1990), Whatley (1993), and Malamuth and Check (1985).

3. My findings for oral and anal rape are higher than Russell's (1990), who found that only 5% of her sample experienced either act; and Finkelhor and Yllö's (1985), who found that 20% of the women in their sample experienced oral-genital sex, and 32% were anally raped. However, my research coincides with Peacock's (1995) findings that 40% were anally raped and 45% were forced to perform fellatio on their partners.

4. In addition to interviewing 50 women about their experiences of wife rape, Finkelhor and Yllö (1985) also interviewed three men who admitted they had used force at least one time to have sex with their wives.

5. Abigail remained with her partner for many years and, although he never tried to sexually assault her again, the emotional abuse continued and was quite extreme.

6. More than two thirds of the women mentioned that their husbands frequently used drugs and/or alcohol; however, only three of the women blamed the substance abuse for causing the rapes. The majority of women in this sample believed their partners would have been abusive with or without substance usage.

3

Defining and
Ending the Violence

In the preceding chapter, we began to explore the complexity of wife rape by addressing the nature of this type of violence and the coping strategies women develop in response to their experiences. The focus of this chapter is on how women define their experiences of wife rape and end the violence. My interviews with wife rape survivors indicate that the processes of coping with the violence, defining the abuse as rape, and ending the violence are all interconnected. For example, if a woman immediately identifies her forced sexual experience as rape, she is more likely to terminate the relationship or take great steps (such as leaving and going to a shelter) to ensure that another attack does not occur. However, if a woman does not perceive her experience as rape, viewing the forced sex as aberrant or minimizing the severity of the assault, she begins to cope with the violence and is less likely to take direct action to terminate the relationship or seek help. Thus, as Adams (1993) writes, naming the violence is crucial: "Victims need to name their world, so that the terror will stop, and so that they will no longer be victimized but will become survivors" (p. 63).

The Importance of Defining Sexual Violence

The question of how women define their experiences of rape is central to this book. To answer this question, my research was grounded in a social constructionist perspective. This perspective begins with the premise that reality is socially constructed (Schneider, 1985). Sociologists who study social problems from this perspective seek to understand how problems are defined and to analyze the "claims-making" activities of experts (Loseke, 1992). However, rather than seeking to understand the definition of wife rape from the perspective of experts, this chapter examines how survivors of wife rape construct their own experiences of rape and define the violence.

This area has been long neglected in the literature concerning violence against women. Kelly (1990) argues that this void is significant because "this often results in the distortion and even exclusion of instances of sexual violence, as it fails to take account of the complexity of how women define and understand their own experience(s)" (p. 116).

Rather than allowing survivors of violence to express themselves, we tend to rely on experts' definitions and interpretations of how women comprehend the violence (Loseke & Cahill, 1984).[1] To date, most studies of sexual and physical violence have merely slotted women into preconceived analytic definitions of abuse without regard to how women conceptualize their own experiences or how they reach the point of identification (Kelly, 1990).

Given the legal history of wife rape and the ambiguous nature of the problem in this society, this is particularly problematic because experts' definitions may not reflect the perceptions of women who have experienced this type of sexual violence. Indeed, several researchers have established that women define their experiences of wife rape differently than experts. Diana Russell (1990) found that 14% of women's described experiences fit her definition of marital rape (oral, anal, vaginal, or digital penetration obtained by force or threat of force, without the woman's consent or when she is unable to consent). However, only 7% of the women defined their experiences as rape. Peacock's (1995) research revealed that only 30% of women whose experiences met her definition of marital rape also defined their experiences as rape. Furthermore, fewer than 40% were familiar with the term *marital rape* prior to their assault. Frieze (1983) found that many women in her study admitted to feeling pressured to have sex with their partners, but they did not construct their experiences as rape. This occurs in part because many women have difficulty applying the word *rape* to their experiences of sexual violence. The reasons for this will be explored in detail later in this chapter.

Thus, we see that the subjective experiences of women who are raped by their partners do not always mesh with the collective representation of wife rape by experts. This has important implications for helping this population, because organizations may be unable to identify or respond to the needs of this group (Loseke, 1992; Russell, 1990; Smith, 1994). We will consider this issue in the following chapters. Now let us turn to the question of how women define their experiences as wife rape.

Defining Wife Rape

According to Kelly (1988), understanding how women define their experiences as rape involves three stages: "Women must define the incident first, as lying outside the normal, acceptable, or inevitable behavior and second, as abusive. Contacting support services or answering research questions involves a third step: naming the experience as a particular form of abuse" (p. 140).

One third of the women ($n = 14$) in my sample immediately identified their experiences as rape. As I indicated previously, six of them were able to terminate their relationships with partners immediately. The others acknowledged that their husbands had raped them, but for a variety of reasons, including financial constraints, fear, and a lack of available alternatives, felt that they had to stay in their relationships.

The majority of women in my sample, however, did not immediately define their experiences as rape and take steps to end the violence. Instead, most used various coping strategies to manage the sexual violence, including reducing their risk of assault and minimizing their risk of injury. These women redefined their experiences as rape over the course of their relationships. Let us consider some of the factors that contributed to this process of redefinition.

Naming the Violence

Kelly (1990) argues that "in order to define something, a word has to exist with which to name it . . . [and] the name, once known, must be applicable to one's own experience" (p. 114). One reason that several women in my sample were unable to define their experiences as rape was because the term *marital rape* did not exist when their experiences began. Because terms such as *domestic violence* and *marital rape* are recent additions into our language, women have historically lacked a social definition that allowed them to see the abuse as anything more than a personal problem (Kelly, 1988; Schechter, 1982). This was particularly significant for eight of the women, all of whom were over 50 at the time of the interview, who considered themselves to be from "another generation."

For many of these women, experiences of sexual violence occurred long before 1975, when states began to criminalize wife rape (Finkelhor & Yllö, 1985). For example, Annabel remembers that when her experiences of sexual abuse first began, "there was no such thing as marital rape. People didn't even talk about regular [stranger] rape. And there certainly weren't any shelters. It was a personal problem." Erica told me that she was first raped "20 years ago, and we didn't have enough insight into things like that." Similarly, Gwenn, the oldest woman in this sample, remembered that after her husband violently raped her, she "never dreamed [that] could be rape. I didn't know a husband could rape a wife." However, when a police officer told Gwenn that husbands can rape their wives and confirmed that her experience was indeed rape, she filed charges against her partner and terminated the marriage.

These quotes reflect Kelly's (1990) argument that the first step in defining experiences of rape is having access to a name. However, this is not enough. For women to construct their experiences as wife rape, they must see this social definition as corresponding to their own experiences of sexual violence (Kelly, 1990). Several women in this study were unable to apply the social definition because they perceived sex in marriage to be obligatory.

Sex as an Obligation

Several of the older women whom I interviewed were initially hesitant to define their experiences as wife rape because they considered sex with their partners to be their obligation as wives. For example, Coral told me, "That was a long time ago, and I didn't know it was rape. I thought I had to because I was his wife—it was my duty."

Russell (1990) reported that there is some evidence of a correlation between age and a belief that wives must submit to their husbands' sexual demands because of the marital contract.

However, it was not only the older women in this sample who initially hesitated to identify their experiences as wife rape because they saw sex as their duty. Several younger women were also hesitant. For example, Sonya recalled that her husband often forced her to have sex, but she said, "I didn't see it as rape. I saw it as my duty. I thought that I should do it because I'm his wife and I should do it because, in my heart, I care about him." In the same vein, Wanda recalled "this confusion about what does a good wife do? I had never been married before . . . and I thought this is your husband and he can't rape you."

This confusion about conjugal rights and women's social role as "good wives" was reiterated by several other women in this study, most of whom were inexperienced with men when they got married. For example, Delilah told me, "I had never been with anyone before, and I didn't know or understand what was normal in a relationship, and nobody ever told me, 'that's normal' or 'that's abuse,' so I didn't know."

Delilah's statement reflects the fact that in the United States, marital sexuality has historically been cloaked in secrecy. Indeed, researchers including Rubin (1976), Blumstein and Schwartz (1983), and Kinsey, Wardell, Pomeroy, and Martin (1953) have all noted the difficulty couples have in expressing their thoughts about sexuality and sexual practices. This secrecy can be problematic because it is often difficult to determine normative sexual behavior in marriage. Indeed, several of the women I interviewed expressed their confusion about what was normal in a marital relationship, thus making it difficult for them to draw a line between consensual intercourse and rape.

Redefining the Violence

Although traditional understandings about marital sexuality and confusion about what constitutes normal relations initially prohibited some of the women from naming their experiences wife rape, most gradually redefined their experience as such. As Ferraro and Johnson (1983) found with their study of battered women, a variety of catalysts, including changes in resources and changes in the relationship, cause battered women to redefine the abuse. My interviews with wife rape survivors revealed that redefinition was most frequently triggered by three factors:

1. The violence approached the level of severity they associated with stranger rape.
2. The violence became abnormal.
3. They received help from an outsider.[2]

Stranger Rape as "Real Rape"

Comparing their experiences to stereotypical stranger rape was one of the most important factors in how women defined (or redefined) their experiences of sexual violence. Although the comparison to stranger rape was significant for everyone in this study, it served as a hindrance to redefinition for some and a facilitator for others.

One reason women were initially hesitant to identify their experiences as rape was because rape has stereotypically been defined as "a rare experience between a woman and an anonymous assailant" (Kelly, 1990, p. 123). The image of an unknown assailant waiting in an alley to attack his unsuspecting victim is so popular that many people have difficulty associating any type of relationship, whether it is a dating or marital one, with the word *rape*. Indeed, the majority of women with whom I spoke said that they initially hesitated to apply this term to their experiences because they thought that rape happened only between strangers, not between people who loved each other. Debbie made a distinction between stranger and marital rape several times during her interview. She explained that she did not feel comfortable seeking help because "my husband did this. If it had been a stranger, I could have talked about it to family or called a crisis center, but I couldn't talk about my husband as if he was a stranger."

Several of the women in this study were prompted to define their experiences as rape when the assaults approached the level of brutality they associated with stranger rape. For example, Stacey was horrified by a particularly brutal incident in which her husband raped her in front of their child and tried to bite off her nipple. She said,

> I couldn't believe it. After he was done, he said, "Thank you ma'am" and left. I had never felt so violated, and I knew that rape by a stranger in the street could not be any worse than this—so ugly and filthy.

Karen also immediately saw her experience as rape:

> It was very clear to me. He raped me. He ripped off my pajamas, he beat me up. I mean, some scumbag down the street would do that to me. So to me it wasn't any different because I was married to him, it was rape—real clear what it was. It emotionally hurt worse [than stranger rape]. I mean you can compartmentalize it as stranger rape—you were at the wrong place at the wrong time. You can manage to get over it differently. But here you're at home with your husband, and you don't expect that. I was under constant terror [from then on] even if he didn't do it.

Several of the women in this study labeled their experiences as rape when the circumstances surrounding the sexual assault were similar to those of a stereotypical stranger rape. For example, three women were kidnapped by their partners, taken to isolated locations, and raped and battered over a period of time. Each of these women had previously been forced to have sex against her will by her partner but applied the label rape to her experience after the kidnap because the circumstances resembled what might happen with a stranger.

For instance, after he dragged her off the street and badly beat and raped her, Pam's partner locked her in a trailer and set it on fire. Although Pam had been physically and sexually abused by this man for 10 years, this experience was so brutal that she immediately contacted the police and filed charges against him for rape and attempted murder. I asked her if she thought that this experience was rape, and she responded, "When someone snatches me up off the street and takes something I don't want to give you—oh yeah—that's rape."

Barbara had been forced to have sex with her partner several times over the course of their violent 2-year relationship. However, she didn't identify her experience as rape until he dragged her to an abandoned warehouse, where he intermittently used crack cocaine and raped her for several days.

Nina also was battered by her partner for several years before the first incident of forced sex occurred. When I asked her if she defined that experience as rape, she told me, "No, because I was with him and he had a right to do that." Nina redefined her experience as rape when they were separated and her partner found her, dragged her into the woods, and brutally assaulted her. Nina told me that she knew this was rape because "I was away from him for about a month or so, and I said no and he took it anyway."

For these women, the fact that they were all taken forcibly to isolated locations and brutally beaten and raped by their partners prompted them to redefine their experiences as "real" rape. Following this final incident, all three women terminated their relationships with their partners, and each of the assailants was sentenced to prison for the assault.

We see that stereotypes about what constitutes real rape kept several women from applying the term to their own experiences. However, many used stereotypes about stranger rape as a measuring rod to redefine their experiences of forced sex as rape.

Changes in the Violence, Changes in Definition

One third of the women in this study did not redefine the violence as problematic until they perceived it as "different" from previous experiences. As Loseke (1987) argues, every woman's construction of what is and is not normal in a relationship is subjectively determined, so each woman's definition of what constitutes rape also varies. Most of the women redefined the violence when it became abnormal in frequency or severity.

As I indicated in the preceding chapter, all of the women in this sample were physically abused at some point during their relationships. For some, this was a rare occurrence, and for others, it was routine. Several women had experienced systematic battering for years, and for them, the physical violence had become second nature. However, when their husbands sexually assaulted them, they perceived this as abnormal and defined the experience as rape. For example, Sally told me,

> He had been physical [physically violent] for awhile, and he just worked it [the rape] right in, just one night he worked it in. There was no warning and no building its way up. . . . I remember thinking it's the same thing as a woman being raped. I remember crying and not being able to leave the bed, and in my head, I knew what I was going through was rape.

Several women perceived the violence as a problem when it became abnormal in its severity. For instance, Lorraine first began to think there was a problem when the attacks became more frequent during her pregnancy. She said, "He got meaner and was into kinkier sex—it became more violent and frequent." Debbie remembered that after several months of sexual abuse,

> it got totally out of hand. I was getting hurt, really hurt, and when it comes to the point where I'm patching up cuts on my body and tears on my body four and five times a day, this is ridiculous. And I knew he had a problem, but then it was so bad that there was nobody to talk to.

Other women applied the term *rape* to their experiences when their partners' sexual demands changed or became deviant by their standards. As I indicated in the last chapter, 40% of the women were sodomized by their partners, and one third were forced to perform oral sex. For several women, such actions were the catalysts for redefining the violence. Sara's experience provides an example:

> I thought he [her husband] wanted to make love because we were kissing, and we took our clothes off. And then my husband rolled me over and drew me up on my hands and knees and put his arms around me and held me real tight and forced himself into my rear end. . . . He pushed himself into me and I was screaming at him to stop, that he was hurting me, and he squeezed me tighter and started going faster. . . . He came in me, and I jumped up and went into the bathroom and started having diarrhea, and that lasted about a week. . . . After that, I knew he had no respect for me. He didn't care about my feelings or what I thought.

Three of the women in this sample were penetrated vaginally with objects such as weapons, feathers, brushes, and various types of food. Natalie identified her experience as rape when "I was getting really hurt . . . and he [her partner] forced a banana into me and I couldn't make him stop." Thus, "deviant" actions or changes in the violence such as these triggered several women's redefinition of their experiences.

Receiving Outside Help

Many of the women did not begin to redefine their experiences as rape until they were out of the relationship, and others initiated the process of redefinition. For example, Dawn attended a meeting where I was speaking about wife rape. Afterward, she approached me and said, "That woman in your story was me, and I never thought it was rape." In another case, Annabel finally left her husband when her last child went to college, but she had not yet defined her experiences as rape. Her turning point came when she recognized herself in the literature on domestic violence, which she began reading after she joined a support group for battered women.

Like Annabel, several women mentioned that self-help literature helped them to clarify their thinking about their experiences. Even more important was the story of John and Lorena Bobbitt, which was highly publicized during my interviews. Several women said this case was central either in their redefining their experiences as rape or in confirming their subjective experiences of rape.[3]

About 20% of the women also mentioned the value of seeing a talk show—*Oprah* being the most influential—for reaffirming their own definitions of their experiences. For example, Melissa recalled,

> I knew it was rape the whole time. I saw it on *Oprah*. He said he would change, but he never did. I got tired of it—12 years is a long time to deal with that [abuse] . . . and I started talking back to him. One time I was watching *Oprah* on battered women, and he got mad and told me turn it off and blamed that "bitch" [Oprah] for my talking back to him.

As Adams (1993) argues, the media are important in helping women to name their experiences of sexual violence because often women lack the language to do so: "But when, through representation and identification, an image is offered by the media, naming pours forth" (p. 64).

Although the media were clearly influential, their contact with service providers was even more important to the women in this study. Indeed, many of the women did not redefine their experiences as rape until they contacted a battered women's shelter or a rape crisis center for help.

In her work on women's help-seeking behavior, Cavanagh (1978) writes that battered women initially contact agencies to talk, have their feelings validated, and discuss ways to end the violence. As their coping strategies fail, women often approach organizations to sanction their violent partners and/or end the relationships (in Kelly, 1988). My research reveals that women did indeed contact battered women's shelters and rape crisis centers for a variety of reasons, and service providers were important in how women conceptualized their experiences of sexual violence.

For example, Wanda had countless negative interactions with support services but found one counselor at a rape crisis center who was instrumental in helping her to redefine her experiences:

> She was the first one who really believed what I was saying, and I would request her or find out when she was around and talk to her. She was very patient and tolerant and a good listener and communicator, and she was very reaffirming. I told her about what was going on, and she said to me, "You know what it is, you answered your own question," and I said, "I'm just looking for someone who does this for a living to tell me from a legal standpoint what's in the state guidelines." She said it was absolutely spousal rape. She went through it with me as I had already perceived it, and she was a big help.

As Ferraro and Johnson (1983) note, shelters are important because advocates have the potential to provide battered women with external definitions of the violence, and thus, they may serve as catalysts to redefine the violence. In my study, several of the women did not begin to redefine their experiences as rape until they entered a battered women's shelter and were asked specific questions about their experiences of forced sex in their relationships. Becky told me,

> I guess I had just figured that abuse was abuse. I don't think I ever looked at it as any other way than abuse, but I was talking to [a staff member] about it, and I asked her if she considered that sexual abuse. She told me it was sexual abuse and rape and that I could press charges against him. I never considered it rape, but then I knew it was a violation of my body.

Like Becky, Lisa did not begin the process of redefinition until she was a resident of a battered women's shelter. After speaking with a counselor and then later sharing her experiences with me during an interview, she said,

> I feel so much better now after talking about it. If someone's studying this, then it's not just me. It's all starting to come together now what really happened to me, and it's not only me who went through this.

Of course, women's definitions of their experiences can be undermined when they do not receive a positive response from service providers. In the following chapters, we will explore in detail the interaction of wife rape survivors with service providers.

Still in the Process of Redefining

Before concluding this discussion, I should note that not every woman in this sample had constructed her experience as wife rape at the time of the interview. In fact, three of the women were actively involved in reconceptualizing their experiences of "unpleasant" or "forced sex" as rape, and their definitions of their experiences were rather ambiguous. Although all three admitted they had not freely consented to sex, they had difficulty verbalizing their experiences as wife rape because their partners were the assailants. For example, Cory, a lesbian, believed that sex was her obligation as a wife, and because she always refused her husband, she thought he had a right to force her. She told me, "I should have slept with him willingly like a good wife, so it's partly my fault." She was actively struggling to apply the term *rape* to her experiences.

Alice, one of the older women in this sample, continued to have difficulty labeling her experiences as rape because she considered herself to be "from another generation." When I asked Alice if she felt that her husband had raped her, she replied,

> I don't use that word because I'm married. I hear it on TV, and it seems funny. He was my husband, so I don't see it as rape unless he beat me up during it or hit me. I feel funny calling it rape.

Although Alice now has the linguistic means to identify her experience, she still does not feel comfortable constructing her experience as rape and instead calls it forced sex.

Last, Rebecca was an advocate for battered women and admitted to being forced to have sex against her will. However, she said she still had difficulty identifying herself as a "victim of rape."

Several of the women in this study evidently had fluid definitions of their experiences—they felt uncomfortable with the terminology of rape, however, they also realized that there was some force involved. As these examples reveal, although women might experience similar acts of sexual assault, their personal definitions and interpretations of the violence vary (Kelly, 1990). Thus, we see the importance of not labeling women's experiences for them but allowing them the opportunity to define their own experiences in their own terms.

The Value of (Re)defining Wife Rape

Adams (1993) writes that "the power of naming is the power of self-authorization" (p. 79). Regardless of when or how the women in my study defined their experiences as wife rape, all of them felt empowered in doing so. For some, the redefinition provided a release from self-blame, and for others, it had an eye-opening effect. Even those who had coped with the sexual violence for long periods of time and had avoided seeing their husbands as rapists felt that redefining their experience was beneficial in allowing them to understand their relationships more completely.

For example, once Debbie acknowledged that she was a survivor of wife rape, she was able to see her husband and their relationship in "its real light—as sometimes violent and not loving." Similarly, Lisa felt that once she defined her experiences as rape, "it started to come together. Now I've started to understand what happened—the rape and why. I'm starting to know it wasn't my fault."

Lisa's quote exemplifies the feeling of empowerment many women have when they apply a social definition of sexual violence to their own personal experiences. Doing so decreases their sense of isolation and self-blame. Kelly (1988) argues that although the process of redefinition is often distressing, it is usually positive in the sense that the survivor's feelings of anger and betrayal (which are often suppressed) are finally validated. With redefinition, these women also felt more in control of their lives, and many made the important step of ending the violence.

Choosing to End the Violence

Although there may be other strategies for ending the violence, all of the women in this study chose to leave their abusive partners.[4] This coincides with Frieze's (1983) and Russell's (1990) findings that leaving their partners is a common behavioral reaction of raped wives.

Several of the women in this study did not find it particularly traumatic to end their relationships. For example, Rhonda and Gwenn were already separated from their husbands, and Karen had been considering divorce at the time of the first rape. Ending the relationship was a realistic option for these women, and, I would argue, this was an important factor in their ability to immediately define their experiences as rape. Here is now Karen expressed her understanding of the connection between defining wife rape and ending the violence.

> They [the survivors] just see it as one more aspect of being battered and don't define it as rape. Because if you acknowledge it as rape, then you have to do something about it. This [rape] is more awful than getting beat up, so how do you explain living with a rapist. So it's part of the problem. If you define it as rape, then you have to do something about it. So it's easier to continue the denial.

Thus, Karen argued that women often fail to identify their experiences as rape if they feel unable to leave the relationship.

For the majority of women in this study, the decision to end their relationship was not an easy one to make. Loseke and Cahill (1984) argue that both the external and internal constraints that victimized women face, as well as the factors involved in any individual's decision to leave, influence whether or not a woman leaves a violent relationship. Several of the women I spoke with mentioned reasons such as new employment opportunities, their completion of a high school or college degree, and children leaving home as enabling them to leave. Others left when they felt their children were in danger. For example, although Tanya had suffered a year of sadistic sexual abuse by her partner, she left when their child was born and she feared that her partner would hurt the infant.

Most women in this sample terminated their relationships as a direct result of the violence. This is significant because, as I indicated earlier, it was frequently changes in the violence that prompted women to define their experiences as wife rape.

About 75% of women in this sample left when the sexual and physical violence in their relationships suddenly escalated. For example, Cory said she terminated her relationship with her husband after "he just snapped and held me for 6 hours in the bedroom and physically and sexually abused me."

Many feared that the escalating violence put their lives at risk. This fear is certainly justified: As researchers (Browne, 1993; Pagelow, 1992) have found, wife rape is characteristic of violent marital relationships that often end in homicide. About 60% of the women in this study said their partners had threatened to kill them. For some, this happened routinely, and for others, this threat was what caused them to end the relationship. For example, Wanda left after her husband held a gun to her head, and Becky left after her husband brutally raped her and broke her ribs. Becky remembered thinking, "In the last 4 months it's steadily gotten worse, and one of these days I'm not going to get out of here. He's going to kill me."

Three of the women in this sample ended their relationships with their partners when the violence had escalated to the point where they feared they might kill their abusers. In her study, Browne (1987) found that three quarters of the battered women who killed their partners reported being raped at least once by their partners. Although more than half of the women in my sample had thoughts, sometimes quite graphic ones, of killing their partners, only three believed they might act on these thoughts. Coral remembered the incident vividly:

> He came home. I had a knife in the kitchen, and he started screaming and yelling, and I pulled out the knife and he backed away. I put the knife to his stomach and cut him some, but I don't know what I would have done if he hadn't stopped, and that scared me. . . . The next morning I said he better leave because I was gonna kill him or he was gonna kill me, and I didn't want that. I didn't like what I was doing—it scared me. So he left.

Coral was frightened enough by her own use of violence to force her partner to leave. However, it was not only her husband whom she held responsible for forcing her to take such drastic steps; she also blamed other members of her community, who had failed her when she turned to them for help.

Seeking Help

Frieze (1983) notes that, compared with women who are battered but not raped, victims of wife rape are more likely to seek help for marital problems. All of the women in this study were asked to whom they spoke about the violence. As I indicated in Chapter 1, all of the women in my sample were recruited based on their contact with women's organizations. However, these women told me they had turned to a variety of sources for support, including religious advisers, family members, friends, and the police, as well as women's organizations.

Religious Advisers

Several ($n = 7$) women sought help from their priests or ministers in ending the violence, and two said they had received positive responses. These women felt their ministers (both of whom were women) were supportive of their decisions to leave their partners and said they helpfully offered phone numbers for local shelters.

However, most of the women were not helped by their religious advisers. For example, Danielle told me,

> I went to a Catholic priest, and I told him what was going on, and he told me I should just stay in this relationship, and I couldn't believe that. I thought, why should I stay if he's abusive? Then I talked to my mother, and she said to stay. I really couldn't believe it.

Karen recalled a similar experience:

> Being Catholic, I talked to a priest who said I should go back if he [her husband] says he's sorry. I was supposed to, but I said I couldn't do it any more. . . . It was emotionally rough because you feel compelled to keep the marriage together, and yet his behavior really dissolves [sic] you of that responsibility because he raped you.

Like Karen, several women felt it was important to seek their religious adviser's support. However, as past research has indicated, support for women in violent relationships is not always forthcoming (Alsdurf & Alsdurf, 1989; Bowker, 1983; Stacey & Shupe, 1983). Indeed, Bowker (1983) found that battered women ranked clergy members at the bottom of the list of those to whom they had turned for help. This is not surprising, given the stigma attached to divorce under any circumstances by many religious institutions. Furthermore, emphasis on wives' responsibility to "obey their husbands" and husbands' divine right to rule their wives reinforces power inequality in marital relationships. Such ideology is clearly related to the perpetuation of wife rape.

As Finkelhor and Yllö (1985) point out, for centuries the Catholic church has taught that it is sinful for women to refuse sexual intercourse with their husbands. Thus, women may acquiesce to sex because they feel that they have no right to refuse their husbands, or they may hesitate to seek help because they feel that their own behavior is sinful. This occurred in the case of Alice, a woman who characterized herself as very religious. She told me forced sex "was just like getting up every morning, it was just part of life as his wife."

For years, Alice did not think she had the right to seek assistance when her husband coerced her to have sex. Similarly, Coral remained in a violent relationship for years and tried to make it work. She was particularly bitter about the church's response to the problem of violence against women. She said, "I blame the church for a lot of it [domestic violence] and for telling women it's their duty [to have sex] and to stay. So when I left my husband, I left the church and God, too."

Certainly we cannot generalize about the response of the entire religious community to the problem of wife rape based on such a small sample, and more research on this question is necessary. However, it is important to note that of the few women who did seek help from their religious advisers, most were dissatisfied with the response they received.

This is problematic, as Adams (1993) argues, because religious advisers are in an important position to reach those women who might not feel comfortable seeking help from women's agencies or others in the community.[5]

Family and Friends

Research on domestic violence indicates that battered women frequently turn to family members for help (Bowker, 1986). However, the majority of wife rape survivors in this sample did not seek help from family members or friends to end the violence. Some said they were afraid to involve people they cared about with their violent partners, and they feared their partners' retribution if they learned that their wives had talked to others about their "private" relationship. Others felt too embarrassed to talk to friends about the sexual violence. For example, Delilah said, "It's not something you can call your girlfriend about and say it's your husband doing this to you."

Debbie felt unable to turn to family members:

> When you're going through this, you can't go to your family. You've got Thanksgiving and Christmas and birthdays, and this is not an issue that's brought up. It's just not. So you're pretty much on your own, and you deal with it as best you can. I think if it were a stranger [who did this], I would get a lot more support.

The primary reason that women in this sample gave for not turning to family members and friends was that they felt isolated and disconnected from their support networks. Indeed, more than two thirds of the women in this study mentioned that their husbands actively tried to minimize their contact with family, friends, or colleagues as a way to keep them isolated and under control. For example, Cory remembered being "like a prisoner in my own home. I couldn't go outside and nobody could come in." Natalie recalled similar feelings:

> He kept me locked in the house, and the Dobermans were in the backyard so I couldn't get out—I was afraid of his dogs. I was like incarcerated. He wouldn't let me talk to my family or friends, and I really hate him for that.

Although the majority of women in this sample felt disconnected from their support networks, one third were successful in contacting friends, and one quarter were successful in contacting family members for assistance. Most of the women who told friends about the violence found their reactions to be helpful—usually in the form of providing them with a temporary place to stay or telephone numbers for local shelters. Only three of the women who shared their experiences with friends felt they were disbelieved.

Of the women who told family members about their experiences, the majority received a positive response. Common reactions of family members were to provide financial support, emotional support, or indirect intervention in the form of contacting local women's organizations or the police. This last strategy, although sometimes effective, more often backfired, as Melissa recalled: "My family would call the police on him [her husband], and he would beat me bad for that." Indeed, several women experienced extremely violent beatings after family members tried, unsuccessfully, to intervene.

Although most of the women felt supported by family members, three did not. These women all discussed their experiences with their mothers and felt that their mothers did not believe them. In fact, all three were encouraged by their mothers to stay and work on their relationships. Even after Danielle left her partner, her mother was still focused on their reconciliation. Danielle remembered, "I got a three-page letter when I was at the shelter from my mother saying why did I leave him when he was a good husband and didn't do anything to me? She still believes him."

We see that although a few women experienced negative reactions from family members and friends, most felt positively about the support they were offered. However, we should remember that the majority of women in this sample did not seek support from these sources, as research has indicated domestic violence survivors so frequently do (Bowker, 1986). Instead, women in this sample were more likely to turn to formal sources of assistance, such as the police and women's agencies, to end the violence.

Police

Studies of rape and domestic violence have consistently indicated that both types of crime are highly underreported (see, for example, Adams, 1993; Edwards, 1989; Straus, Gelles, & Steinmetz, 1980). It is estimated that less than 10% of rapes are reported to the police and that the majority of battered women do not report their abuse (Russell, 1990). With regard to domestic violence, most research reveals that the police response has historically been inadequate (Pagelow, 1992; Saunders & Size, 1986). Indeed, police officers often fail to take domestic violence calls seriously, engage in victim-blaming behavior, and sympathize with the abusers (Renzetti, 1992; Straus et al., 1980).

In this study, 37% ($n = 15$) of the women called the police for help on at least one occasion. For three other women in this study, calling the police for help was not a viable option because their partners were affiliated with the police department.[6] About 80% of these women were not satisfied with the police response to their calls.

Most commonly, women felt that the police were unresponsive to them because the abusers were their husbands. Erica "couldn't believe it. They [the police] were no help at all because we were married." Pam told me,

> I called the cops one day, and they came and said, "You gotta go" and made *me* leave. And I said, "I called you, and you're taking his side." They were his friends, and they didn't care that he beat me up. It was my fault.

When Donna called the police for assistance, they encouraged her to "work it out and get marital counseling." Donna never called the police again. In Becky's case, the police referred her to a battered women's shelter; however, they later informed her husband where she was. As a result of the danger this posed to both herself and the other women in residence, Becky was forced to relocate to another shelter.

The women in this study talked particularly about the lack of police interest in their complaints of wife rape. This is consistent with the findings of other researchers. Russell (1990) found that 19% of wife rape survivors in her study reported the violence to the police, but few were adequately helped. Frieze (1983) found that only one third of her sample found the police helpful. Indeed, Frieze (1983) argues that police officers are even less responsive to wife rape victims than they are to battered women. My interviews reflected the lack of positive police response to complaints about wife rape.

For example, Sally called the police on one occasion after her husband brutally raped and battered her:

> The police wouldn't come out, and when they did, they didn't even take the knife [that her husband had used to assault her], and they didn't want me to press charges. I wanted to have a rape kit done and asked for a woman, and they said there was no woman. There was no one to speak to me.

Wanda met with a similar response: "The police wouldn't let me do a rape kit, and they said we don't know about that law [against wife rape]." Because of the police reaction, Wanda did not pursue filing charges. In fact only eight women in my study saw their husbands charged with rape in the criminal justice system.[7] At the time of their interviews, four of the women's partners were serving time in prison for assaulting them, one's husband was missing, and three were awaiting court dates.

Of those women who did file reports with the police, only two found police officers supportive. Most had experiences similar to Sally's:

> I had to go to the state police, and then I had to go through three detectives and explain everything and be totally embarrassed, and I had to talk about penises and how he ejaculated and how he did certain things. I had to do it with the [tape] recorder on, and they kept saying, "Could you say that again miss, speak up, miss, and call it this and that, miss." And "what kind of underwear were you wearing, miss? Were you wearing fancy negligees?" They were like his [her husband's] buddies, and they were busting my balls. They should have been more qualified to handle this case, and they should have a woman in that situation.

Indeed, Sally and many other women in this sample did not think the police treated their complaints of wife rape seriously. Therefore, many stopped calling the police for help.

Several women were quite persistent and contacted the police on numerous occasions, only to find that their calls were never treated seriously. For example, after a particularly brutal incident, Paula called the police:

> I saw the cops walking up the walkway, but they never came in. I know today that I should have sued the police department, because I could have been lying there almost near death, and I saw two officers walk up and then turn around and leave and then I was like, I knew I was dead. He [her husband] was going to kill me for calling the police, and he was very violent all that day, and I stayed in the bedroom all day petrified.

Natalie also called the police repeatedly but eventually stopped because the police routinely "did nothing" and her partner would beat her unmercifully to punish her for her "betrayal."

In one case, Karen was finally able to successfully obtain the help of the police when she cleverly disguised the nature of the problem. Karen had called the police on numerous occasions and said it normally took them 45 minutes to respond to her calls. With her past experiences in mind, on the day she left her abuser, Karen

> called the cops and said some guy was beating up some lady in front of the house with a gun. They first asked me if the guy was married to the woman—like that makes a big difference. I said no and they showed up in 15 minutes.

With the reluctant help of the police, Karen was able to escape her abuser. However, we see that most of the women who contacted the police found them to be uninterested and unresponsive to their complaints of domestic violence and/or wife rape.

The experiences of these women highlight the need to improve the response of police officers to the problem of wife rape. One option is to provide better education about wife rape. As Russell (1990) argues, the police should be educated about the reality of wife rape; confronted with sexist attitudes that assume women are the property of their husbands; and taught not to engage in victim blaming by immediately identifying with husbands. Another solution suggested by Paula is to hold police departments accountable for their nonresponsiveness. As Dobash and Dobash (1979) argue, women have been successful in challenging police department policies on domestic violence by filing individual as well as class action lawsuits. Such action may be necessary with regard to wife rape because of the critical role the police can play in helping women to end the violence.

A positive response from a police officer can have an important effect on how a woman perceives the violence and the choices she makes about ending the violence. For example, police told Gwenn that her experience was rape, and they encouraged her to file a complaint against her husband. She did so and immediately left her husband.

Russell (1990) argues the need for more women police officers and for their involvement in cases of domestic violence and rape in order to more adequately and sensitively respond to the needs of wife rape survivors. It is important for police officers (regardless of gender) to raise the issue of wife rape routinely when they respond to calls of domestic violence. The woman in this study who felt most positive about the police's response to her call was Rhonda. She said, "I went to the police, and they said I had the wrong complaint—it wasn't just assault but sexual assault. . . . And there was a female officer, and she said to file a complaint and everything would be OK." Unfortunately, most of the women in this sample did not have such a positive experience with the police and turned instead to other sources of assistance to end the violence.

Shelters and Rape Crisis Centers

Two final sources of support for women in my study were battered women's shelters and rape crisis centers. Researchers such as Cavanagh (1978) and Schechter (1982) have noted that battered women's shelters are important resources for assisting women in ending the violence in their lives. Indeed, half of the women in my sample entered a battered women's shelter upon leaving their partners, and all had sought help from service providers to cope with the violence, end their relationships, or recover from their experiences of wife rape.

Although some of the women were clearly helped by service providers, particularly to end the violence, the majority did not feel that their problems as survivors of wife rape were fully addressed. The most common criticisms were that their experiences of wife rape were ignored and that they did not feel they fit into the agencies' agendas.

The response of service providers to wife rape survivors and women's perceptions of agency services are the topics of the next two chapters. However, before moving to these issues, I want to briefly consider the effects that wife rape had on the women in this study.

The Effects of Wife Rape

None of the women I interviewed escaped from their marriages totally unscathed, nor have they fully recovered (the time lapsed since the violence ended ranged from 1 to 14 years). This is not surprising; many researchers (Campbell, 1989; Finkelhor & Yllö, 1985; Hanneke & Shields, 1985; Resnick et al., 1991; Russell, 1990) have documented the severe consequences associated with being raped by one's partner. Physical effects are often serious and may include "nausea and vomiting, soreness, bruising, muscle tension, headaches, fatigue, and injuries to the genital area" (Adams, 1993, p. 73).

Campbell and Alford (1989) note that wife rape survivors also commonly suffer from vaginal stretching, miscarriages, stillbirths, bladder infections, and sometimes infertility. Short-term emotional effects often include anxiety, shock, intense fear, depression, and suicidal tendencies (Russell, 1990). In my sample, many of the women talked of suffering from severe depression, and three were hospitalized as a result of this. More than half of the women mentioned considering or attempting suicide at some point.

Within the larger society, and even among service providers, there is a myth that wife rape is somehow less traumatic than rape by a stranger because one's partner is a "known entity." The reality is that survivors of wife rape seem to suffer even more traumatic consequences than stranger rape survivors (Finkelhor & Yllö, 1985; Russell, 1990; Whatley, 1993).

In this sample, all but three of the women suffered long-term effects, including prolonged periods of depression and increased negative feelings about themselves.[8] Many of the women admitted they still suffer from serious problems as a result of the sexual violence.

Rhonda is among the most visibly traumatized by the rape. She lives in constant terror of her husband's return and has physically structured her environment for protection. She does not leave her house at night, carries a butcher knife at all times, and does not speak into the telephone until the caller is identified. She told me, "I live in constant fear of him [her ex-husband]. All the time. And every day I think of how to kill him, and I pray to God it doesn't happen."

Stacey felt that she does not "have full control over [her] mind," and Edna called herself "one of those funny-farm ladies." Debbie said, "I got out with my body first, and my mind came later. It's been 2 years, and I'm still not sure it's all there."

Like other survivors of sexual assault, many of the women in this sample commonly experienced flashbacks and ongoing nightmares about their assaults (Koss & Harvey, 1991; Russell, 1990). Sara said she reached the point where "I felt sick and I couldn't eat for a couple of days. I wasn't sleeping and I was having flashbacks a lot, so I went into the hospital for a few days." The long-term effects suffered by wife rape survivors possibly occur because they frequently experience repeated assaults and, as Browne (1987) argues, "the closer the relationship between rapist and victim, the more violent the sexual assault tends to be" (p. 97).

Wife rape survivors also suffer serious effects because of the bond that they have with their assailants. The majority of the women in this study talked about their inability to trust other men and their fear of intimacy as a result of being raped by their partners. For example, Sonya told me, "I lost part of me. I think part of me deep inside died." Other women talked about how degraded and dirty they felt about the sexual violence because the assailant was someone they had loved. Terri felt "used—like a toilet, like he shitted on me." Sara talked about how filthy she felt, saying she "couldn't get clean."

A common concern expressed by many of the women in this study was that they would experience long-term sexual dysfunctions. Natalie, who was particularly distressed about this, said,

> Now I try to think about sex, and if I even touch myself—my privates—I feel pain and just the thought of a man touching me . . . just makes me crazy. I know something's not right because I get so angry. I know I need help so I can get better.

Lorraine sought help: "The sexual abuse really hurt me, and I started seeing a sex therapist. I was able to transcend those problems with [her new partner]."

Thus, we see that the majority of the women in this sample suffered severe consequences as a result of being raped by their partners. Far from being a trivial incident with minor effects because the assailant is a known entity, we see that wife rape has serious short- and long-term effects for women.

Becoming a Survivor

Despite the horrors that the women in this sample endured, all of them were proud of the fact that they have survived. Indeed, all are survivors in the sense that they became active agents in coping with and ending the violence in their relationships. Mills (1985) describes survivors as women who do not dwell on their victimization and who "have more positive identities and fewer negative identities to draw on in formulating a definition of the self" (p. 118). Several of the women in this sample exemplify Mills's (1985) definition. Lorraine describes herself as feeling

> really strong and positive about myself. Spiritually, I feel like I've transcended all the problems and I'm starting to look at ways to address the unfinished parts—transitions are awful, but I feel like I'm ready again to be an important part of life, and that's a good feeling after wanting to die.

Annabel said that as soon as she left her husband, she felt "like a new person after 29 years. Alive and free and finally not frightened anymore." Annabel is a woman whose primary roles were wife and mother for the longest period of time, yet she has developed new dimensions of her identity since ending her violent relationship, including "becoming a feminist and thinking of going to law school to help other women."

Several of the women I interviewed felt particularly positive about the directions their lives have taken since they terminated their abusive relationships. As one survivor, who is an activist, told me,

> I gave a lot and got a lot back from women who have had the same experience. Most women have this trauma and can't make it right for them, and that's part of the healing. You need to turn it around and make it work for you.

Kayla is an example of someone who has done this:

> A lot of good stuff came out of this [abusive relationship]. It made
> me a stronger person, and now I take care of Kayla, and that's hard
> work. . . . I know it also prepared me for my work. We have to teach
> people to be 100% responsible for your own self. You have to be
> smart and safe and don't depend on other people.

Kayla is a survivor in the sense that she has taken her abusive relationship and transformed it into a tool to help her work with troubled
teenagers.

Like Kayla, many of the other women in this sample have also
made their experiences "work for them." Twelve have become advocates for other victimized women, and two have been actively involved
in campaigning to change the legislation on domestic violence and sexual
assault. Thus, we see that the majority of women in this sample have
not only coped with their experiences of wife rape but have indeed
become survivors in the true sense of the word.

It is important to note that the women who would characterize
themselves as survivors or would meet Mills's (1985) definition of
survivor have all worked hard to develop this identity. Some have
relied on support networks composed of family members and friends.
Others received support from advocates and/or support groups. Kayla
told me her counselor "helped me to believe in myself and helped my
self-esteem, and I have a great network of friends. But a lot of the
work was done within." Regardless of how they have developed their
identity as survivors, it is significant that these women have done so,
and this is a true testimony to the strength and resiliency of wife rape
survivors.

Summary

In the past two chapters, we have seen that wife rape is a serious
problem with very real consequences for the women who experience
it. The ways in which women cope with the violence and interpret
their experiences are not static, but change as their relationships
progress. We have seen that women, far from being passive, are active
agents in manipulating their environments, defining their experiences,
and changing their victim status. In understanding the perspective of
women themselves, we see them resisting at the height of oppression—
physically and mentally—the sexual violation by their husbands. We

also see the limitations of their resistance; that few strategies are effective in protecting them from their assailants. Thus, we explored how women sought help and ended the violence in their lives. In so doing, our goal was to facilitate a greater understanding of the complexity of wife rape and the serious effects of this crime.

In the following chapters, we shift our focus from women's experience of wife rape to the question of how service providers respond to these survivors. In Chapter 4, we look in detail at how a battered women's shelter and a rape crisis center meet the needs of this population. Chapter 5 explores the larger response of women's organizations to the problem of wife rape and considers policy implications of this research.

Notes

1. Loseke and Cahill (1984) define *experts* as a diverse group of people explicitly committed to speaking on behalf of victimized women, including social workers, lawyers, shelter workers, sociologists, and psychologists.

2. Often their redefinition was triggered by a combination of factors; for example, when a woman experienced a change in the level of violence and then sought the help of a service provider who confirmed her definition of her experience.

3. These women were uniformly supportive of Lorena and applauded her courage to do something (sever her husband's penis) that many had wanted to do to their partners.

4. However, following their interviews, two of the women reconciled with their husbands.

5. For a detailed discussion of the clergy's response to wife rape and suggestions for change, see Adams (1993).

6. One woman's partner was a police officer, and two others were police informants.

7. Although most women did not file criminal charges, 60% of them sought restraining orders against their partners. However, few said they were encouraged to do so by the police. Instead, most were assisted by advocates for battered women.

8. Of the three who said they experienced no effects from their experiences of wife rape, two said they just don't think about the relationship or the violence, and one told me that she was more concerned with the effects of the physical abuse rather than the sexual abuse.

4

The Response of Two Agencies to Wife Rape

Emily's Story

Early one winter morning, the hot line rang and a counselor at a battered women's shelter answered it. The caller was a frightened woman named Emily, who was living in an unheated garage with her six children and was looking for shelter for a few days. Emily had been raped by a stranger and also physically and sexually abused by her partner. At this time, she was seeking shelter because the stranger who had raped her had just been released from prison, and she felt that she was in danger. The battered women's shelter was full that morning, so the counselor referred Emily to the local rape crisis center and several other area shelters for assistance.

Later that afternoon, I was collecting data at a rape crisis center when a staff member received a call from Emily. While explaining her history of victimization, Emily described being raped by a stranger and sexually and physically abused by her husband. After Emily explained her situation, the director was contacted regarding her request for shelter. Emily described what she was told: "I called [the rape crisis center] and they couldn't help me. They told me they didn't have any openings [for shelter] and gave me another number to call." The reason that Emily was denied shelter was written in her file: "Per [the director] I explained we were unable to take her because we don't handle domestic violence." After writing this, the staff member who received the call turned to another worker and explained, "It was a domestic violence case, but she knew we were a rape crisis center, so she talked about the rape." Emily was referred back to the battered women's shelter, and a few days later, when space became available, she was accepted into the shelter as a battered woman.

I later interviewed Emily as a survivor of wife rape, and she explained her frustration at how she had been treated: "I called all over the place and nobody was helping me. It [the rape] had happened some years ago, but I felt like it was yesterday because the pain was still there and the anger was still there." Emily's primary concern was finding a safe place for herself and her family, because she was frightened by the release of the stranger who had raped her. Although she had experienced multiple assaults, she felt that she still suffered the most trauma from the stranger rape: It was that experience she continually relived in her flashbacks and nightmares. Indeed, Emily's subjective reality was that of a victim of stranger rape who was in need of assistance. Theoretically, she should have been the perfect candidate for shelter and services at the rape crisis center. However, because of her experiences of sexual and physical violence with her partner, her subjective reality of rape did not conform to the official definition of *rape victim* at the rape crisis center. Thus, she was redefined as a victim of domestic violence and referred to the agency responsible for this problem.

Once at the battered women's shelter, Emily was treated as a battered woman. She was defined as a victim of wife abuse and, although the sexual abuse was noted in her file, the staff focused on the physical abuse, not her experiences of rape. She was grateful for the shelter and safety she and her children received, but Emily was not satisfied with how the shelter addressed the issue of rape:

> The majority of them [other residents] are here for abuse and that's it. But I'm here for a bigger problem [wife rape and stranger rape]. . . . I hate that women's group. I'm just not comfortable in it. I'm just sitting there and like, I'm blank.

When Emily left the shelter, it was noted in the daily log that she "feels very upset and mistreated by us." No other details were provided.

Emily's case indicates the practical realities commonly faced by survivors of wife rape because their experiences of violence do not neatly fit into the agendas of either rape crisis centers or battered women's shelters. As Donileen Loseke (1992) argues, "In modern day America, there are no social services organized to help *any* person to do *any* thing. . . . Organizational form, ideology, and method of service provision each [are] justified only for [one] type of person" (p. 159).

Because there are no shelters or crisis centers that exist solely to provide services to survivors of wife rape, this population must be negotiated into the agendas of other agencies. The problems Emily faced—being shuttled from one organization to another, feeling uncomfortable discussing her experiences of sexual assault, and believing that her issues were not fully understood—were experienced by many of the women I interviewed. These problems are the result of ineffective strategies used by service providers to manage wife rape survivors, and they stem from the fact that the organizations do not claim ownership of the problem of wife rape. Gusfield (1981) defines the sociological concept of ownership as

> "the ability to create and influence the public definition of a problem." This occurs when your construction of a problem gains acceptance, when you become the authority to whom people turn, and when you assume effective control over social policy. (p. 10; quoted in Best, 1990, p. 12)

In this chapter, we will compare how the problem of wife rape was managed by two specific organizations—a battered women's shelter (Refuge) and a rape crisis center (WASA) and consider the reaction of wife rape survivors to the services they received.

The Organizations

Refuge and WASA are nonprofit agencies established during the 1970s or early 1980s to meet the needs of women who were survivors of violence. Both are located in the same county, which is important: Theoretically, they have similar funding constraints, an identical pool of potential employees from which to draw, and the same general population to serve. Thus, these are comparable organizations to analyze.

A more difficult question to answer is, how do these organizations compare with others in the United States? Certainly these organizations resemble those depicted in other research (Gornick, Burt, & Pittman, 1985; Loseke, 1992; Rose, 1977; Schechter, 1982). Furthermore, based on my survey of service providers in the United States, both Refuge and WASA are similar to other battered women's shelters and rape crisis centers with regard to their mission statements, scope of services, and the types of assistance they formally offer to wife rape survivors. The rigidly controlled organizational structure at WASA may make it atypical of other rape crisis centers, as I will explain shortly. However, WASA resembles other mainstream rape crisis centers in terms of its staff size, training programs, and how services are provided to victims of sexual assault and the community (Gornick et al., 1985). Thus, closely examining how Refuge and WASA manage this population may provide important information for understanding the response of other organizations to the problem of wife rape.

Refuge

Refuge is part of a larger women's organization that was established during the early 1900s to "build a fellowship of women and girls" (agency literature). Today this umbrella organization provides a variety of services, from self-help groups to athletic programs for women in the community. As an individual agency, Refuge was founded in the early 1980s with the help of local activists, to provide services such as emergency housing, food, and advocacy to abused women. Today Refuge has become one of the largest shelters in the state; its 30-member staff provides residential services to about 500 women and children each year. Among the residents of Refuge are not only battered women, but also other women and children "in crisis," such as those who are temporarily and chronically homeless. Refuge offers a variety of services to the community, including counseling (both individual and support groups), a 24-hour hot line, advocacy, court preparation and accompaniment, and educational programs on domestic violence. Although its nonresidential program enables Refuge to provide services to an additional 1,500 women and children each year, the main focus of its staff continues to be the women and children in shelter.

The staff of Refuge is composed of women diverse in age, educational level, ethnicity, race, and religion.[1] During the time of my data collection, Refuge had three general categories of employees. The management team consisted of the director and five other individuals who had various responsibilities, including supervising the hot line and volunteer program and monitoring the provision of direct services in the agency. The counseling staff was composed of trained professionals who provided emotional support to the residents in the form of individual and group counseling. The frontline workers, who constituted the largest segment of the agency's staff, were those women most directly involved in meeting the daily needs of the residents of Refuge by providing transportation, food, housing assistance, and general support.

The majority of staff members at Refuge were committed to the mission of the agency, which was not only to provide battered women with a safe environment, but also to empower them and help them to change their lives. Indeed, at Refuge, like so many other shelters for battered women, the goal was to resocialize battered women to "produce strong and independent women" (Loseke, 1992, p. 33). Implicit in this goal was a collective understanding about the type of person who needs to become strong and independent and whom Refuge seeks to help; a battered woman type.

Toward a Collective Representation of Wife Rape

Social constructionists believe that social problems do not merely reflect objective conditions but are socially defined (Blumer, 1971; Hilgartner & Bosk, 1988). This societal definition "gives the social problem its nature, lays out how it is to be approached, and shapes what is done about it" (Blumer, 1971, p. 300). Loseke (1992) argues that these societal definitions are also used as interpretative devices by those involved in the reproduction of public problems. In her study of a battered women's shelter, Loseke (1992) writes that a collective representation of the social problem *wife abuse* among shelter employees helps them to make sense of their work. Using Durkheimian terms, Loseke (1992) defines collective representations as "publicly standardized images of conditions and types of people" (p. 41). For example, within shelters,

[Wife abuse] is a label for severe, frequent, and continuing violence that escalates over time and is unstoppable. Such violence is that in which unrepentant men intentionally harm women and where women are not the authors of their own experiences which they find terrifying. (Loseke, 1992, p. 20)

Shelters were created to meet the needs of a battered woman type, and workers serve as gatekeepers in reproducing this problem by admitting into shelter only those women who fit their collective definition of *victim*.

At Refuge, the collective representation of a battered woman largely reflected Loseke's (1992) depiction. The workers at Refuge perceived their agency as an avenue of escape for the battered woman type of person who was experiencing severe emotional and physical harm as the result of terrifying violence. However, my interest was not in how battered women were processed at Refuge, but in how this agency provided services to a different type of person—a survivor of wife rape.

It is a complex task to unpack the collective representation of wife rape among workers at Refuge, largely because wife rape has not been specifically included in the agency's agenda. Since opening its doors, Refuge has had a formal policy of providing beds to rape survivors in need of shelter; during the mid-1980s, Refuge reserved two beds specifically for rape survivors. For the past several years, the agency has included survivors of domestic violence *and* rape survivors among those who are formally given top priority for receiving assistance. Consequently, 91 survivors of wife rape received assistance from Refuge during the 2-year period I studied.

Although the agency has provided assistance to rape survivors for years, victims of wife rape have not been singled out as a specific population to be granted services, and the problem of wife rape has not been addressed in agency literature or in their outreach programs. Furthermore, at the time that I began my data collection, the vast majority of staff members had received no formal training on the subject of wife rape.[2] Indeed, most of the staff received their information about the topic from private reading, the media, and their interaction with women in the agency. So whereas workers could look to agency literature and their training materials for definitive statements on the objective reality of wife abuse and how this population should be managed, such an objective reality was not so clearly defined for wife rape (Loseke, 1987).

Furthermore, although the management team clearly saw survivors of wife rape as included in their mission to "help women end the violence in their lives," this message was not systematically conveyed to the frontline workers. Thus, there was no uniform understanding of the social construction of wife rape at Refuge.

In general, staff members constructed wife rape either as a different type of problem and thus, out of the realm of Refuge's services, or as a domestic violence problem for which the agency should take responsibility.

Wife Rape: Not Our Problem

Although most Refuge employees were willing to argue that wife rape was a serious problem, and most maintained that battered women were sometimes raped, one third of the staff members (all of whom were frontline workers) constructed wife rape as a problem for rape crisis centers, not battered women's shelters. They argued that Refuge should not be responsible for this problem for two main reasons. First, they argued that these women did not fit the agenda of the agency; rape victims were not battered women and a rape crisis center should handle this problem. This was evident in the following statements made by workers:

> I think they should go to a rape crisis center or WASA. Let them deal with it—they have counselors. That's what [WASA] stands for—[Women Against Sexual Assault].

> They're [staff at the rape crisis center] trained in rape and that's what they specialize in—rape. We do battering.

These workers understood wife rape to be a qualitatively different type of problem than wife abuse. Indeed, the argument here was that wife rape was a rape type of problem, not a battering type of problem, and these women required different services than Refuge offered. This sentiment was expressed by one of the frontline workers:

> I feel [that] a woman who has been raped has different needs; she needs a rape kit and to get some counseling, and there are a series of things I'm sure that should be provided for them that we may not be able to provide here because we deal with victims of domestic violence. I feel they need other things. I'm sorry, but they do, they need different services than what we give here.

This quote also reflects the second reason that many frontline workers gave for not handling the problem of wife rape. That is, they felt inadequately prepared to deal with this issue, and they believed that wife rape survivors would receive better services from an agency trained specifically on the topic of rape. One worker said, "Rape crisis centers should handle it [wife rape]. They're used to dealing with it. People are sick if they force sex—they are sick people, and WASA is better to deal with it."

There was also a perception among these staff members that this population was more fragile and vulnerable than battered women, and therefore, they required more attention and support. As one staff member told me, "Victims of marital rape need more attention than the others because there's just something different about them—like many of them have anxiety attacks and they need more support." I would argue that this "neediness" posed a problem to frontline workers, who already felt overworked trying to manage battered women and homeless women in the shelter. Because raped wives were constructed as a different and more needy type of victim than battered women, these workers denied ownership of the problem and argued that the problem should be handled by another kind of agency.

Wife Rape: A Domestic Violence Problem

Two thirds of the staff members at Refuge believed that wife rape was a problem commonly faced by battered women and an issue for which Refuge should take responsibility for handling. Included in this group were the director of Refuge, her management team, the counseling staff, and half of the frontline workers. These staff members felt that Refuge should claim ownership of wife rape because it was a domestic violence type of problem. One worker told me,

> The mission of Refuge is domestic violence, right? And marital rape is part of domestic violence, so we should handle it.

Similarly, the director said,

> I see marital rape as part of sexual violence and domestic violence. . . . I think we should shelter them here.

Many of the staff members argued that Refuge should be responsible not only because wife rape was a violence-against-women issue,

but also because it was the agency best equipped to handle this population. As a member of the management staff told me,

> Our program is on a much higher level than other agencies that do
> this work. As opposed to [a homeless shelter], we have an under-
> standing of abuse. As opposed to WASA, we have an understanding
> of shelter. Those things are important for marital rape victims—other
> agencies don't do it all.

The director agreed that Refuge should publicly claim ownership
of the problem of wife rape; however, she was hesitant to do so because
of funding constraints and because of the existence of WASA—the local
rape crisis center. Others in the community believed that WASA was
the agency primarily responsible for providing services for all rape
survivors, including wife rape survivors. This was not the case; Refuge
provided more services than WASA to wife rape survivors during the
2-year period I studied. However, for Refuge to publicly claim wife
rape would be interpreted by the director of WASA and others in the
community as an invasion of WASA's "turf." The director of Refuge
was hesitant to do this because WASA and Refuge were the only two
women's agencies that provided services to victims of violence in a
conservative county. Indeed, she preferred to maintain a unified front
and did not want it to appear that the women's agencies were fighting
over money. Thus, although the director of Refuge informally provided services to survivors of wife rape, she did not publicly claim
ownership of wife rape as a social problem. Ultimately, this disjuncture
manifested itself in confusion among staff members about how the
problem of wife rape should be handled.

Managing Wife Rape at Refuge

As indicated earlier, Loseke (1992) argues that shelter workers
have a collective representation of the social problem *wife abuse* that
serves as a tool enabling workers to identify this type of person and
permit them access to the institution created to meet their needs—a
battered women's shelter. Collective representations have a second
important function, and that is to serve as organizational devices (or
schemes of interpretation) allowing workers to make sense of their
daily practical experiences with this population (Joffe, 1986; Loseke,

1992). It is the collective definition of the problem of wife abuse and the battered woman type that enables workers to make sense of their work, manage the problems, and justify their actions. For example, if a woman has numerous curfew violations because she has been seeing her abuser, this is not "appropriate" behavior for a battered woman type (someone who is trying to escape the abuse and become independent), and a worker's decision "to exit her" from the program is viewed as legitimate. In the absence of such collective representations, it is more difficult for staff members to make sense of their work.

Such a collective representation of wife rape was missing at Refuge. This was evident in the confusion that frontline workers expressed with regard to how to manage this population. For example, two frontline workers told me,

> I don't know what to do when they [victims of wife rape] call. Do we bring them in if there are only a few beds left or not?

> I don't ask women about rape only because I don't know what our policy is in regard to that. And they [management] never asked us to mention the sexual abuse part of it.

Although the director included survivors of wife rape in the larger agenda of the organization, this information was not systematically conveyed to frontline workers in the form of written policy. Furthermore, the messages that advocates received from management were perceived as confusing.

The current management team believed that Refuge workers should actively manage the problem of wife rape. However, according to several staff members of Refuge, a former manager (who left shortly before the beginning of my data collection) instructed staff "not to talk with the women but to direct them to the counselors." This manager was particularly concerned about the "emotional fallout" that accompanied rape, and she advised other staff members not to discuss this issue with the women.[3]

In the absence of a formal policy or a group consensus about the nature of the problem and how it should be handled, workers lacked the tools to help them make sense of this population. Consequently, the primary strategy for managing wife rape survivors was to treat them like the population the workers understood so well—battered women.

Managing Wife Rape Survivors as Battered Women

At Refuge, survivors of wife rape were accepted into shelter primarily as survivors of domestic violence and were managed as battered women. In doing this, workers largely ignored the women's experiences of sexual abuse and negotiated their identities so that they fit the organization's collective representation of victim.

This strategy is understandable, given that two thirds of the staff constructed wife rape as a domestic violence type of problem. Furthermore, all of the women I interviewed fit the collective representation of a battered woman, in that they had experienced escalating physical and/or emotional abuse, as well as sexual abuse. Thus, in a sense, they were battered women. The problem is that their experiences of sexual abuse were significant to them, and this issue went largely unaddressed when they were managed as battered women. Before addressing the implications of this, I will analyze how these women were processed at Refuge.

The survivors of wife rape first came into contact with Refuge, as do the vast majority of women, through the hot line. Many of the women called to discuss their violent experiences or to ask for legal advice, whereas others sought shelter. During this initial contact, a woman began her transformation into a battered woman type of person.

When women first called the hot line at Refuge, they were asked direct questions about their history of abuse, but not specifically about sexual abuse.[4] Indeed, it was not the policy of Refuge to include a question on wife rape on the intake form. Unless a woman chose to mention the sexual abuse herself, her experiences of wife rape were likely to go undocumented; 95% of staff members did not regularly ask questions about this. Thus, a victim of wife rape entered the shelter labeled as a battered woman type of person, which was the "appropriate" victim for an agency such as Refuge.

Once they entered the shelter, residents were provided with a variety of services to meet both the physical and therapeutic needs of a battered woman, such as support in locating a home; help in applying for public assistance and/or finding a job; accompaniment to court for legal proceedings or to medical appointments; and emotional support. Although the process of finding a job or a home clearly does not differ on the basis of the type of violence one has experienced, women who have been raped by their partners do have different medical and legal needs. For example, a rape survivor who is thinking of pressing charges is normally encouraged by the police to go to a hospital for a rape kit. This is an extensive procedure in which evidence is collected for prosecutorial purposes. Theoretically, staff members of Refuge could accompany a resident to the hospital for this procedure. However, they were not trained in the specifications of this procedure or its significance. Consequently, in their interviews, many staff members expressed their discomfort with this process and advocated contacting rape crisis counselors to accompany women to the hospital. As one frontline worker told me,

> I think WASA would be more helpful to women in the hospital situation, and they would be there so that tests are correctly done, so you could use that later on in legal proceedings. I think WASA would be better than us because we're not trained to do that.

This also happened with regard to legal advocacy. Although most staff members were well versed in domestic violence legislation, they were not as knowledgeable about the legal status of wife rape. This became apparent during my interviews, when several frontline workers asked me questions about the legal status of wife rape in the state and the success rate in prosecuting cases. Furthermore, when I asked them what advice they give to survivors of wife rape, the majority of workers told me "the same as a battered woman."

A final important service provided to residents of Refuge was emotional support. In this respect, survivors of wife rape were most obviously treated as battered women types; the sexual abuse was largely ignored by frontline workers. In their interviews, only a handful of workers said they brought up the issue of rape with shelter residents when they were providing support. Indeed, many of the workers told me that they did not feel comfortable addressing this issue, even when the residents brought it up. One frontline worker said,

> When they [survivors of wife rape] came here, I didn't say anything to them about that unless they brought it up because I'm not experienced in that, and I wouldn't want to say anything wrong. I don't push when they talk about rape. I leave it at that.

My interviews revealed that many of the workers were uncomfortable with issues of sexual violence, and their discomfort prohibited them from providing emotional support to these women.

During their stay at Refuge, residents were provided with emotional support, not only by frontline workers but also by a trained counseling staff that offered individual and group counseling sessions. During my observations, two groups met regularly in the shelter: a drug/alcohol education group and a women's group that covered a variety of issues concerning domestic violence. Notably, there was not a support group for wife rape survivors at Refuge. Although the issues of childhood sexual assault and wife rape were sometimes raised by the residents themselves in other groups, a support group dedicated to sexual abuse did not exist. This was problematic from the perspective of the survivors of wife rape because they felt uncomfortable and believed their issues were neglected when they were in support groups with battered women who had not been victims of rape. This point will be elaborated upon shortly.

We see that in their efforts to manage this population, workers at Refuge transformed victims of wife rape into the appropriate type of victim for the agency—a battered woman—and often ignored experiences that set them apart from the typical residents. However, several staff members did provide these women with specialized services and addressed their needs as survivors of wife rape.

Managing a Wife Rape Survivor

One of the ways staff members addressed the problem of wife rape was to incorporate questions about sexual abuse into the initial intake form so that women were given the opportunity to speak about their experiences of rape from the onset. Only two staff members regularly asked about sexual abuse. One of the members of the management team told me,

> I ask as part of the history of abuse. And a lot of women will say no.
> . . . I don't phrase it any different or use a different tone than when
> I ask about emotional abuse. I try [to] be concerned, and I just throw
> a question out there, and a lot say flat out no. But I think it's helpful
> to people to have the opening to say yes, if that's the case.

It is significant that this staff member was responsible for documenting one third of the 91 survivors of wife rape who contacted Refuge during a 2-year period. Clearly, asking specific questions about this type of abuse is an important strategy for identifying and providing services to wife rape survivors.

At Refuge, several staff members provided extra support to wife rape survivors with regard to their legal needs. For example, one frontline worker who spent a great deal of time talking with battered women about their experiences and legal issues told me,

> When I suspect sexual abuse, I spend more time with her and that comes out. I spend extra time with that woman so she will feel comfortable talking about it. Sometimes that's why she wants a restraining order, but she doesn't want to say it.

Similarly, one member of the management team (who was the person most likely to accompany women to the police station or to court) was particularly concerned with the issue of marital rape and sensitive to the needs of this population. In her interview, she told me,

> The . . . police are the worst about marital sexual assaults. You have to tell your story to the people outside the detectives' offices and then you have to stand in the middle of a crowded room and tell your story to a detective. I go with the woman [who is sexually assaulted] to make sure she has some privacy and so they [the police] listen to her.

Thus, these Refuge employees were successful in negotiating specialized services to meet the legal needs of wife rape survivors.

A final area in which specialized services were occasionally provided to wife rape survivors was counseling. Although there was no support group specifically for wife rape survivors, several members of the counseling staff were aware of the needs of these women and made individual attempts to provide services. As several counselors told me,

> Well, oftentimes, they didn't tell it to me as abuse, and they would describe the episode, and I would be the one to help them put the language to the experience.

> I know that women don't feel comfortable talking about it [wife rape] so I try to do it on a one-on-one basis with them.

Thus, several counseling staff members negotiated services for survivors of wife rape primarily in the form of providing more individual counseling to address the sexual violence. In doing so, they were able to legitimate the experiences of these women and help them to redefine the violence as rape.

It is evident that some members at Refuge were involved in negotiating services for wife rape survivors; however, the primary strategy was to manage them as battered women. This was the case primarily because workers, lacking a collective definition of the problem of wife rape, managed clients in the way most comfortable for them: as battered women.

In contrast, we see that at WASA, survivors of wife rape were not likely to receive services at all. Although workers shared a collective representation of this problem, agency policy mandated that these women be referred elsewhere for assistance.

WASA

WASA was founded more than 20 years ago as one of the first rape crisis centers in the nation. During this stage of the anti-rape movement, the objectives were to provide emotional support to survivors of rape and help them to navigate the criminal justice system. As Rose (1977) notes, rape crisis centers were originally developed to provide 24-hour emergency hot lines and information about medical and legal procedures to rape survivors. Like staff at other rape crisis centers, WASA members initially provided telephone support to survivors of rape. With increases in funding and membership, WASA expanded beyond providing hot-line counseling to offer a variety of services for survivors of rape, including escorting victims to local hospitals and police departments and providing rape prevention programs to the community. WASA also recently built a shelter to provide temporary housing for survivors of rape.

Compared with Refuge, the local battered women's shelter, WASA was a much smaller agency. At the time of my data collection, WASA had a full-time staff of seven, including the founder, who was also the president/chief executive officer; three administrative employees; and three "counselors/speakers," who handled the majority of hot-line calls and community presentations. Whereas members of Refuge were quite diverse in terms of age, class, and race, this was not the case at WASA. All of the employees were middle class, and with the exception of one, all were white.

The most striking difference between Refuge and WASA was that, although Refuge was organized hierarchically and the director clearly had the authority to make important policy decisions alone, she rarely did so without guidance from both the management team and front-line workers. Refuge was generally perceived by the staff and the larger community as a feminist organization, empowering not only its clients but also its workers. In contrast, WASA was strictly hierarchical in its organizational structure, and the president/CEO has been responsible for determining policy, securing funding, and providing leadership for the organization since its inception. The president of WASA was responsible for determining the agenda of the agency, and this had important implications for the workers and how they managed certain populations, such as survivors of wife rape.

The Social Construction of Wife Rape at WASA

As I indicated previously, workers' collective definitions of problems and organizational goals are relevant to how social problems work is done (Loseke, 1992). From its origins, the mission of WASA was clear to those involved in the organization: to support victims of sexual assault. However, there were important ideological differences between how the president of WASA and her staff interpreted this mission with regard to survivors of wife rape.

At the time of my data collection, the president of WASA did not construct wife rape as a serious social problem that her agency should be responsible for addressing. I would argue that there were two reasons for this. First, she considered wife rape to be less serious than stranger rape, the problem her agency was created to address. In a conversation, she told me, "Marital rape is just not as traumatic as other forms of rape. Your husband is a known entity, so it's not so bad. We're more focused on other issues here." This was reiterated by an employee, who said,

> I don't think [the president] sees marital rape as a problem. I think she sees it as that's her husband. In the wee small hours of 2 to 4 some time, she may see it as a real issue, but I don't know that she sees it as as big an issue as it really is. I think she sees stranger rape as a big issue, and she may see date rape possibly, but I don't think she puts marital rape on that same level because she really hasn't advanced past what she did 20 years ago. And 20 years ago, folks weren't talking

about marital rape. Twenty years ago they were talking stranger rape, so that's why that's very vivid in her mind.

A second reason the president of WASA denied ownership of the problem was because she ultimately constructed wife rape as a form of domestic violence and, therefore, as not her problem.[5] That the president did not claim ownership of domestic violence became obvious in two notations made in client files. In one incident, a woman called to describe her experiences of sexual and physical abuse and to seek advice. The president answered the call and noted in the file, "counseled her about going public and who would be affected if she did—children etc. . . . She was battered." Although it was documented in the file that this woman had described experiences of sexual abuse, the president labeled her case domestic violence and referred her to a local shelter.

In a second example, a staff member received a crisis call from a woman who had been raped and battered by her partner. The notation in her file read, "Per [the president] I explained we were unable to take her because we don't handle domestic violence. I referred her to Refuge." The message workers at WASA received was that the president was not concerned with wife rape. As several staff members told me,

> She [the president] doesn't see it as a real issue because it's your husband. The agency [WASA] doesn't take it seriously. It's not an issue we're supposed to deal with. It shouldn't be bottom-drawered, and I think it is here.

This lack of ownership was apparent in the fact that, at the time of my data collection, there was no outreach in the form of brochures on wife rape or presentations by staff members specifically on this issue. This is in contrast to presentations and brochures that directly discuss stranger rape, date rape, and incest. Notably, wife rape was not mentioned once in any of the agency literature or in the mission statement. Clearly, the president of WASA did not make any public claims about the problem of wife rape, nor did she construct it as a serious rape problem her agency should address.

In contrast to the president, the staff of WASA shared a collective definition of wife rape as a serious social problem. This may reflect the fact that prior to the period of my official data collection, I suggested that a component on marital rape be added to the 40-hour staff/volunteer training program.[6] The president agreed that I could provide new members with information on date rape and marital rape.[7] Although most of the staff members had gone through my training program, the president of WASA had not. Thus, it is quite plausible that having a greater understanding about sexual and physical violence contributed to workers' collective representation of wife rape at WASA.

All six of the staff members believed that wife rape was a serious social problem and were willing to claim ownership of this issue. As one worker told me,

> I think it happens a lot. A lot more than what's reported, and until recently nobody even talked about it. See, it goes against what most people think of as marriage, to think of rape in marriage, and I can't even begin to think of how many unreported cases there are.

The staff members of WASA perceived rape as a problem that *battered* women commonly face; however, they also acknowledged that this was an issue their agency should be responsible for addressing. Several said,

> They're [victims of wife rape] in crisis, and we should counsel them to help bring them out of it.

> WASA is one of a few places in the whole area to give them the kind of [emotional] support they need. Even social agencies, if they don't deal specifically with rape, they may not have a full grasp of the myths about rape and the truth, and if they're not around it every day, they may not be able to support them. I think [Refuge] would be a good resource for them . . . but at the same time they would need a lot of help with the marital rape situation, and I don't know how they handle that there.

Although the staff at WASA was willing to claim ownership of the problem and provide services to this population, the president was not, and this had important implications for how these women were managed at WASA.

Managing Wife Rape at WASA

We saw that, at Refuge, survivors of wife rape were primarily treated as battered women. At WASA, the primary strategy was to shuttle these women elsewhere for services. The term *shuttle* was eloquently used by a woman I interviewed to describe her experience of being referred from place to place for services. The practice of shuttling occurred at WASA not because workers did not consider this a serious problem for which they should be responsible, but because this was agency policy. However, we will see that workers were sometimes successful in negotiating services and treating these women as victims of a particular type of sexual assault—wife rape. We will explore both of these strategies as they were used at WASA.

Shuttling Survivors of Wife Rape

At WASA, women who called regarding their experiences of wife rape were most frequently referred to other agencies for assistance. Of the 40 women I interviewed, 14 contacted WASA at some point for assistance. Seventy-two percent of these women were not provided with services but were referred to other organizations, such as battered women's shelters and victim advocacy programs. My content analysis of agency files reveals that this was not unusual but indeed the norm for wife rape survivors.

During a 2-year period for which I analyzed the agency files, WASA staff members documented 56 calls from women who claimed to be raped and/or battered by their partners. Of this total, 29 women (52%) were directly referred to other agencies for assistance. Most were referred to Refuge, and the others were told to call another area shelter, counseling program, or state agency such as a victim/witness program for assistance. From the files, it is unclear what support was offered to these women before they were shuttled to other agencies. Of the remaining cases, it is evident that WASA workers provided some assistance, at least in the form of crisis counseling. Five of these women received hospital escorts and were then referred to area shelters for support. Thus, approximately 60% of wife rape survivors who contacted WASA for support were ultimately shuttled to other agencies.

One might argue that an organization like WASA, a rape crisis center with its own shelter, would be uniquely qualified to provide services to survivors of wife rape. Indeed, this agency seems tailor-made for a person who requires shelter, advocacy, and support for sexual abuse. However, this was not the case.

My analysis revealed that not a single survivor of wife rape was provided with shelter at WASA during a 2-year period. At Refuge, women were often turned away because of insufficient space.[8] At WASA, space was not the problem. According to WASA's 1993 Agency Annual Report, only one woman was sheltered for several days during that year. As several workers reiterated, the shelter at WASA was never used:

It's never used. It doesn't serve any population.

To my own personal knowledge, it's never been open.

I've been here a year, and there's been nobody who's stayed here since I've been here.

At Refuge, individual frontline workers had the autonomy and discretion to bring women into shelter; WASA workers did not. In fact, workers at WASA had so rarely seen anyone accepted into the shelter that they lacked a collective definition of who might be an appropriate applicant. As one staff member told me,

I don't know what the guidelines [for accepting victims] are. I know I never saw an actual outline of what the procedures are, except I know it's a short-term shelter and women can't use any drugs or alcohol and there's no type of abuse situation. [Why?] Because [the president] will say we [the staff] can't deal with that, and the volunteers can't deal with that.

Although the staff members at WASA were not clear on who might qualify as an appropriate candidate for the shelter, they were certain that a survivor of wife rape would not be deemed appropriate. Because wife rape was constructed as a domestic violence type of problem at WASA, the informal policy of the agency was that these women should be referred to battered women's shelters in the area for housing and counseling. As several staff members told me,

When victims of marital rape call, I think they're referred to [Refuge] all the time.

When a victim of marital rape calls, I discuss whether she feels [that] leaving is an option for her, and she needs to be making the decision. And if she says she wants to leave but has no place to go, I would refer her to a shelter.

The institutionalization of this policy of shuttling wife rape survivors became particularly apparent to me during two incidents. During one training session for new staff/volunteers, someone asked what she should do when a marital rape victim calls on the hot line at night looking for shelter. A staff member responded, "It's routine to call Refuge. Especially on nights and weekends. They have a 24-hour hot line." During another training session, a young woman asked about receiving counseling calls from battered women. A staff member told her, "We don't counsel for battering. If someone calls to talk about abuse, we have to immediately give them a referral to a shelter." This practice is problematic for wife rape survivors because they often call and address the physical violence first before feeling comfortable enough to discuss the sexual abuse. With this policy in effect, it is likely that many survivors of wife rape were denied services.

We see that survivors of wife rape were shuttled elsewhere not only for shelter but also for counseling. Although crisis counseling was the service for which WASA was most known, and they provided this service to survivors of date rape, incest, and stranger rape, wife rape victims were commonly denied this service and referred to battered women's shelters for support. My analysis of agency files revealed that most wife rape survivors who called over a 2-year period were shuttled to other agencies for counseling. Furthermore, although WASA offered support groups for survivors of incest and other forms of sexual assault, no such group was offered specifically for wife rape survivors. One employee told me that women who were raped by their husbands were not permitted to attend support groups at all but instead were referred elsewhere for help.

Thus, we see that the primary way of managing survivors of wife rape at WASA was to shuttle them to battered women's shelters for assistance because they were not included in the agency agenda. In most cases, these women were treated as battered women, rather than survivors of sexual assault, and deemed inappropriate to receive services.

Providing Services to Wife Rape Survivors

It should be noted that some survivors of wife rape were provided with assistance at WASA. This occurred when support could be negotiated by individual staff members by circumventing agency policies. The primary service received by wife rape survivors at WASA was support at local hospitals. This service was provided to all rape survivors, regardless of whom their assailant was.[9] As previously indicated, five survivors of wife rape were escorted through medical procedures by WASA staff members during the 2-year period of my data collection.

The role of WASA staff members in accompanying women to the hospital was to provide emotional support and ensure that evidence was accurately collected for use in prosecuting the rapist. WASA staff members provided support to wife rape survivors as they would to anyone else: They discussed the rape kit with them and provided crisis counseling. One staff member said, "Well, they're in crisis then, so we just try to keep them calm and tell them everything is going to be OK and make sure they know they're not to blame."

As another staff member's experience reflects, women who have been raped by their partners may need even more support than other rape survivors because of the negative treatment they often receive by medical care providers.

> I had red lines in my hands for days after because I was so furious at how she [the raped wife] was treated by the doctor, and I knew there wasn't anything I could do. [What happened?] She [the doctor] came into the room and asked her [the victim] why she was there. She said for a rape kit, and the doctor told her it wasn't really rape, and it was her fault for staying in that situation when they [the couple] weren't sexually active any more.

In this case, the wife rape survivor particularly needed the extra support a rape crisis counselor could provide.

In conclusion, we see that WASA workers were occasionally able to negotiate services for survivors of wife rape. The service recipients were those who fit into the agency agenda and did not require special services, such as shelter, extensive advocacy, or counseling specifically for wife rape. This type of person would have needs similar to the average client of the agency; thus, services could easily be rendered to these women.

However, women with "special needs" did not easily fit into the agency agenda at WASA; they were most likely to be shuttled elsewhere for support. Ultimately, this is where problems occurred, because there were no resources within this community created to meet the specific needs of this population. At best, wife rape survivors were worked into the larger agendas of existing agencies such as

Refuge as battered women. At worst, they were shuttled from one agency to another because they were labeled inappropriate for assistance.

As we will see, most survivors of wife rape whom I interviewed found these strategies unsatisfactory and felt that their issues were not adequately addressed. Before concluding this chapter, let us consider the reactions of the survivors of wife rape themselves to the services they received at Refuge and WASA.

Women's Responses to Service Providers

The experience of Emily, depicted in the beginning of this chapter, was not unlike that of many wife rape survivors I interviewed. Like most of the other women, Emily believed that she did not neatly correspond to the collective representation of *victim* at either a rape crisis center or a battered women's shelter because she had been raped by her partner. Ultimately, most women I interviewed felt their needs as survivors of wife rape were not met by the agencies to whom they turned for help. In their interviews, women discussed the problems they encountered when they were shuttled from one agency to another or incorporated into the organizational agenda as traditional clients.

Shuttling Survivors of Wife Rape

Many of the women in my study received a similar response when they contacted a service provider for help. As several told me,

I didn't fit their [a rape crisis center] image of a good victim. I had been battered for years, and they didn't know what to do with me.

They [a rape crisis center] told me that they don't get funds for domestic violence and that I should call a battered women's shelter.

I called [a rape crisis center], but they said they don't get grants for wife rape. Just for victims of stranger rape and date rape. And if it's your husband—I don't know. They don't know how to deal with it, and they don't get any money for that. They think only rape by a stranger or date rape is rape. Until their grant covered it, I wasn't in their category. Women who are raped by their husbands don't have nothing.

Because these women did not fit the ideal type of victim at these agencies, many were sent from one service provider to another. Wanda says that she was shuttled between dozens of agencies as she looked for helped. She told me, "I've been screwed by every agency in the area. Nobody would help me." Sally contacted so many service providers that she lost count and ultimately concluded that because she was a victim of wife rape, she was destined to get the runaround. In an extensive monologue, she told me,

> Everybody just tries to push it [wife rape] under the rug. It's still not considered a social crime. You can't freely talk about it or admit what happened. . . . In my case, sure, he went to prison, but how many women know that they can do that, how many women know that they can speak up and that something will be done? How many women know that if they went into the police barracks, they would be believed? . . .
>
> Sure, you have shelters for wife abuse, but you don't have a shelter for wife rape, you don't have anything that's being done, you have zip. They tell me to make another phone call, and that's nothing. Everybody is like yeah, yeah, yeah, leave, leave, leave, and nobody will help you.

This process of being shuttled from one agency to another ultimately led Sally to call Refuge and say, "I was a battered woman, but I don't want to talk about that. Is there someone there who can deal with rape?" Sally was not alone in her frustration at the failure of agencies to take responsibility for this problem. However, this strategy of shuttling not only is problematic because it is frustrating to survivors of wife rape; it can also be dangerous.

There are several reasons that shuttling can be a dangerous practice. First, my interviews with 40 survivors of wife rape revealed that (re)defining their experiences as rape is an important step for women in ending the violence. We know that survivors of wife rape often have difficulty defining their experiences as rape and that women's agencies play an important role in this definitional process. Denying a woman services and referring her to other agencies may indicate to her that her problem is not a serious one; that she is not worthy of public sympathy. Thus, shuttling survivors of wife rape who call for assistance is problematic because in doing so, workers often fail to legitimate women's experiences, facilitate the definitional process, and help them to end the violence.

Battered women's shelters and rape crisis centers play an important role, not only because they help women define their experiences of sexual violence, but also because they provide survivors of wife rape with options. As other researchers have noted, it often takes great courage for women in violent relationships to reach out for assistance (Hoff, 1990; Martin, 1976). The same is true for wife rape survivors. These women often blame themselves for their own sexual inadequacies or for failing to manage the violence successfully. They may be too embarrassed or humiliated to seek help, or they may be uncertain that their experiences are real rape. For all of these reasons, survivors of wife rape may be hesitant to disclose their victimization (Finkelhor & Yllö, 1985; Hanneke & Shields, 1985). Given this, it can be dangerous for service providers to cut off dialogue with a woman because she is not the appropriate type of victim for their agency.

Remember that it was the policy of WASA to cut off survivors of domestic violence and refer them to shelters. Two service providers I interviewed addressed the problems associated with this practice:

> They [battered women] get cut off and don't make the next call, and that's real important because your first contact with the client is going to be the determining factor in the continuing treatment, and you can really provide or not provide that support and cut her off for another 10 years. And you tell her to make another call and that's so discouraging.

> When a victim of domestic violence calls, we cut them off and refer them, and I think that's a problem because it's tough to make that first call, and if all that leads to is another referral, then you have to sit and face the phone again and try to make another call.

This problem was echoed by Sally, a survivor of wife rape: "Say a woman makes a mistake and calls a rape hot line and they give her the song and dance that I got. She might not pick up the phone again."

These comments indicate the danger involved with this practice because it silences the woman who is in a violent relationship. This is what occurred with Debbie: "All I needed was someone to say, 'OK, you need help, it's not your fault.' Instead I was laughed at and told [by a counselor] that my husband couldn't possibly rape me." Debbie remained in the violent relationship for a long period of time after this incident.

Shuttling women to other agencies can also be dangerous because it requires that they make additional phone calls. For some of the women who were isolated and had limited opportunities to call for help, such as Natalie (whose partner monitored the phone bills and regularly called home when he was away to see whether or not she was using the phone), this increases their risk of detection and decreases the likelihood that they will be able to escape. Thus, the practice of shuttling not only fails to validate women's experiences of wife rape, but it may also potentially endanger their lives.

Treating Wife Rape Survivors as Traditional Clients

Incorporating wife rape survivors into the organizational agenda as normal or traditional clients of the agency was the strategy most frequently used by Refuge workers. Furthermore, as I will discuss in the following chapter, this appears to be the most prevalent strategy among the service providers who responded to my survey. Indeed, two thirds (75%) of the respondents indicated, at some point in their surveys, that they did not differentiate between wife rape and other types of violence in their provision of services.

Although one could argue that this is good because we should treat rape as rape or all acts of domestic violence as domestic violence, this practice is not without problems. Failing to differentiate between types of violence is problematic when the specific needs of a population are not addressed and when the experiences of women are not legitimated as wife rape but confounded with other types of violence.

Research indicates that survivors of wife rape have emotional needs that differ from those of battered women who are not sexually abused. Many researchers (Campbell, 1989; Hanneke & Shields, 1985; Weingourt, 1985) have documented the serious effects that being raped by one's partner has on women's self-esteem, body image, and mental health. Furthermore, others have argued that being raped *and* battered by one's husband causes even more severe long-term effects than just being battered; these include lower self-esteem, sexual dysfunction, increased general fear of men, and increased negative feelings toward men (Campbell, 1989; Russell, 1990; Shields & Hanneke, 1983).

Among those women who experienced both battering and rape in my study, rape was considered to be the most significant problem, not the battering. Finkelhor and Yllö's (1985) research reveals similar findings. They argue that the sexual abuse seemed particularly traumatizing to women because "beatings seemed more external, and the physical injuries they cause soon disappear. But wives who were raped often comment on the more personal, intimate nature of the sexual abuse: the psychic wounds it left felt deeper" (Finkelhor & Yllö, 1985, p. 135). When treated as battered women, the wounds left by the sexual abuse often go unaddressed.

Although most of the women I interviewed were assisted by service providers in leaving their partners (and half entered a battered women's shelter), most were processed as battered women. These women generally felt that service providers had played an important role in helping them to end the physical violence and cope with the trauma caused by battering. However, a primary complaint of these women was that their experiences of sexual abuse were ignored by staff members once they entered a shelter.

For example, Wanda told me that she felt neglected because she was raped but not physically battered prior to coming to the shelter. She said,

> I don't know if they looked at me if my problems weren't as significant as some women who come in beat up. Maybe they thought my problem wasn't serious because I didn't come in with bruises all over me. Now [the director] said to me, "We look at abuse as abuse," but the rest of the staff I didn't know about. You get conditioned, and I'm sure hardened to all of this after awhile, and you get numb—it's just another client who walks in the door—here are your sheets, towels, and all right, breakfast is tomorrow, and you're left with this numb feeling inside.

In another case, Natalie told me upon leaving the shelter,

"I still got problems, especially sexual problems. I didn't know who to talk to here because I know [a staff member] does housing and so on, but no one came up to me to talk about this." As we can see, these women had a need to discuss their particular experiences of sexual violence.

Many survivors of wife rape felt that although their problems of sexual violence might not have been ignored, they were not completely understood by others at the battered women's shelter. Barbara told me that she did not feel comfortable sharing her experiences with the other women in shelter or with the staff because "I feel like I can't talk to anyone about my relationship—nobody understands it and nobody even asks me about it. I just don't feel comfortable talking about it, and I should feel comfortable here, right?" Shortly after this conversation, Barbara transferred to another battered women's shelter in a different state. Similarly, Cory told me that she felt less comfortable sharing her experiences of sexual abuse with the staff because "it's easier to talk about the physical because it's more accepted and they [the staff] understand that."

Nowhere was it more apparent that wife rape survivors felt misunderstood than in support groups. Most did not feel comfortable sharing their experiences with battered women in a group setting because they felt "different" than others. For example, Barbara said, "It was like the other women were just staring at me. They knew and I knew that beating was bad, but this [rape] is just worse. So I stopped talking about it." Similarly, Danielle told me this about the battered women's group she attended: "They [the other women] were smacked or something like that. But I was the only one sexually abused at the time. So it was hard to talk about it."

Most of the women in this sample who attended a support group at a battered women's shelter had a similar response. They expressed a sense that their problem was somehow different and more embarrassing than that of the other women in the group, and they did not feel comfortable sharing their experiences of sexual violence. Indeed, the most common complaints that survivors of wife rape made about Refuge's services were that they wanted a support group specifically for sexual violence and that they wanted more individual counseling to help them heal. Both of these comments indicate that what these women really wanted was to be treated as survivors of wife rape.

Summary

We see that there are important implications that result from the strategies commonly used by service providers to respond to wife rape survivors. Shuttling women not only results in their often feeling neglected and isolated; it can be quite dangerous to women's physical safety. By merely incorporating this population into the existing organizational agenda, women's specific needs as wife rape survivors are often ignored and their feelings about the sexual abuse may go unresolved. Thus, the end result is that survivors of wife rape often feel neglected, isolated, and/or uncomfortable with service providers, the very people who should play an important role in helping them to recover from the trauma they have suffered.

In the following chapter, we will see that the organizational responses to wife rape presented here are not isolated occurrences but indicative of the response of women's agencies in general to this problem. The final chapter discusses the results of a survey sent to battered women's shelters, rape crisis centers, and combination programs across the United States; it addresses ways in which agencies can improve services to survivors of wife rape.

Notes

1. Among the staff members, there are 14 African American, 12 white, and 4 Hispanic women. The ages of the staff range from 22 to 65.

2. Since completing my data collection at Refuge, I have organized a training program on wife rape for both volunteers and staff members. This training program emerged out of the director's request that her employees become better educated on the topic and that the agency take a more active role in helping this population.

3. This manager was concerned that women would become highly upset recalling their experiences of sexual abuse and that the frontline workers would be incapable of providing adequate emotional support to them.

4. At one time the intake did contain questions about sexual abuse; however, the previously mentioned manager, who feared the "emotional fallout" of discussing rape, campaigned successfully for the removal of these questions.

5. It could be argued that the president of WASA failed to take responsibility for addressing the problem of wife rape because of constraints imposed on her agency by state funding agencies. However, as Matthews (1995) indicates, there are a variety of ways, such as apparent accommodation and overt opposition, by which rape crisis centers commonly resolve conflicts with funding sources.

6. The state requires that agencies give crisis counselors 40 hours of training so that volunteers and staff members can provide women with confidential services. At WASA, the 40-hour program includes general medical and legal information about rape, as well as specific sessions on molestation. These training sessions serve as major sources of indoctrination for new members into the norms of the organization.

7. Although this training was valuable because the staff was provided with more information about this topic, the president enacted no policy changes to include wife rape survivors in the agency agenda.

8. Agency records indicate that each year, hundreds of women and children are turned away from Refuge because the shelter is full.

9. When calls from the emergency room were received, the only question normally asked was whether or not the woman wanted a representative of WASA there to support her. Information about the assailant was not generally taken; thus, it is likely that the staff member or volunteer responding to the call would not know of the relationship to the assailant until she met the woman at the hospital.

5

Providing Services
to Wife Rape Survivors
Current Trends and
Future Directions

The goal of this book is to provide a better understanding of how women experience wife rape and how service providers respond to this problem. In the preceding chapters, the focus has been on women's experiences of sexual violence. We have seen that wife rape is a serious problem with very real consequences for the women who are violated by their partners. No typical depiction of wife rape emerges; women's experiences vary in terms of the number of incidents, degree of force used, and types of unwanted sexual behavior. The strategies women use to cope with the sexual violence also vary considerably. Although some women are raped once and immediately end the violence, others are raped countless numbers of times over the years and try to manage the violence by minimizing their risk of being assaulted and seriously injured.

We have seen that survivors of wife rape often have difficulty defining their experiences as rape. They may see sex in marriage as their obligation, or laws and stereotypes about "real rape" in this society may hinder their ability to name their experience wife rape.

However, it is valuable for women to (re)define their experiences as wife rape, not only because they often find it empowering, but also because doing so is often the catalyst for change. Having redefined their experiences as rape, many women decide to end the violence. We have seen that wife rape survivors turn to a variety of people for help in ending the violence, including the police, family members, and service providers.

Understanding the response of service providers to wife rape survivors is a major focus of this book. In the previous chapter, we saw that neither WASA nor Refuge had publicly claimed ownership of the problem of wife rape or implemented extensive policies and practices to specifically address the needs of this population. Instead, WASA routinely shuttled these women to other agencies for assistance, and Refuge workers incorporated them into their agenda as battered women. The wife rape survivors whom I interviewed generally were dissatisfied by the responses they received and felt they did not "fit" into the agenda of either agency.

In this chapter, we will see that the organizations I studied are not the only ones that have failed wife rape survivors. As others (Russell, 1990; Thompson-Haas, 1987) have noted, women's agencies in general have failed to take responsibility for dealing with the problem of wife rape. Indeed, my research reveals that many organizations throughout the United States are not providing services to wife rape survivors, and these women are falling through the cracks.

The Survey

Between December 1994 and March 1995, I conducted a survey of 1,730 service providers; this included all of the battered women's shelters, rape crisis centers, and combination shelter/rape crisis centers in the United States that were listed in two major directories. Of the 621 service providers who responded, 41% represented combination battered women/rape crisis programs, 32% were battered women's shelters, 22% were rape crisis centers, and the remaining 5% were university-based crisis intervention programs, hot lines, or legal advocacy offices. Analysis of the responses reveals that although most agencies say they provide some services to survivors of wife rape, most do not provide comprehensive services to meet the specific needs of this population nor have they claimed ownership of this issue.

The Response of Service Providers to Wife Rape

The survey revealed that battered women's shelters and rape crisis centers frequently fail to provide several services to survivors of wife rape. One such service is outreach. About 34% of responding agencies provide no outreach to wife rape survivors themselves or educational programs on this problem. When outreach is done, it most frequently takes the form of providing brochures that mention wife rape and presentations that include some reference to this issue. Fewer than 5% of the responding agencies indicated they provide brochures specifically on the subject of wife rape and/or presentations to the community that focus on this issue.

Another serious deficiency is providing education to staff members and volunteers about wife rape. Almost a decade ago, Thompson-Haas (1987) conducted a survey of women's agencies and found that 40% of battered women's shelters, 72% of sexual assault programs, and 77% of combination shelter/rape crisis programs provided staff training on wife rape (Russell, 1990). My recent survey reveals little if any improvement—62% of respondents indicated they provide training to both staff and volunteers.[1] However, there is significant variation among the types of agencies and their provision of wife rape training. For example, 79% of rape crisis centers and 72% of combination programs currently provide training on this topic to both their staff and volunteers. However, only 42% of battered women's programs train both their staff and volunteers on wife rape. That less than half of battered women's programs provide this training is a problem, given the research (see Chapter 1, this volume) indicating that battered women are particularly at risk for being raped by their partners (Browne, 1993; Campbell, 1989).

When training is provided, one third of the agencies (33.5%) educate their staff and volunteers about a variety of important issues, including the legal rights of wife rape survivors, available resources for them, emotional reactions to sexual abuse, and how to identify this population. However, most agencies fail to address a critical issue in their training programs: how to effectively counsel survivors of wife rape and help them to recover from the trauma(s) they have experienced.

The absence of counseling technique training is particularly relevant given that counseling wife rape survivors is a service overlooked by many agencies. This is exemplified by the fact that 98% of service providers do not offer a support group specifically for survivors of wife rape. Indeed, of those who responded to my survey, only eight agencies indicated that they offer a group specifically for women sexually assaulted by their spouses.[2] Furthermore, 25% of battered women's programs offer shelter to survivors of wife rape but do not provide them with individual counseling to further the healing process. Thus, we see that service providers often neglect to offer basic services, such as counseling for wife rape survivors and outreach and training on this topic.

Claiming Ownership of Wife Rape

There is also evidence that most service providers have not claimed ownership of the problem of wife rape. Less than half (42%) of service providers even ask women about experiencing wife rape. Furthermore, my survey found that only 4% of service providers specifically refer to the problem of wife rape in their mission statements. Although 68% of the responding agencies include wife rape survivors under the larger headings of sexual assault survivors or battered women, this problem is not specifically claimed by most agencies. Furthermore, 26% of the service providers responded that wife rape survivors are *not* included in their missions. There were several reasons offered for their failure to own this problem.

One of the most popular reasons given by service providers is that wife rape is not "their problem." When asked why wife rape survivors were not included in the mission, many respondents wrote, "We are a domestic violence shelter" or "We are a rape crisis center;" thus, they imply that this is not a problem their particular agency should have the responsibility to address. This understanding is evident in the following comments, written by representatives of battered women's shelters when asked to explain why they did not provide services to survivors of wife rape:[3]

> We are not staffed to service rape victims, so we refer them to a rape crisis center.

> The counselors aren't trained in sexual abuse, but we make referrals to the appropriate agencies.

> We would refer the client to another agency that works with sexual assault victims.

> We screen victims, and if there is a case of marital rape, we seek more professional advice and counseling from other agencies.

> Normally sexual assault cases are referred elsewhere for counseling.

Implicit in these responses is an understanding similar to that held by one third of the staff members at Refuge—that wife rape is a different type of problem than domestic violence and that battered women's shelters are not equipped to handle this issue. Indeed, this construction of wife rape was particularly evident in the response of one service provider: "If the victim is experiencing marital rape and domestic violence, we treat the domestic violence issues and refer [her] to a rape crisis center for rape." As I indicated in the previous chapter, there are serious implications of shuttling women elsewhere for services. Equally problematic is what Karen, one survivor of wife rape, referred to as "chopping up" the experiences of women by sending them to multiple agencies to address their experiences of wife rape. This point will be elaborated upon later in the chapter.

Another primary reason that agency representatives gave for failing to provide services to wife rape survivors or to include this problem in their mission statement is that this population makes up an insignificant portion of their clientele. One respondent replied, "We've never gotten a report or call concerning marital rape." Another wrote, "I have worked here 5 years, and I have never received a call for marital rape. We are a small county." Finally, one service provider wrote, "We never receive calls for marital rape—[we're a] small county of 14,000; maybe they don't understand marital rape issues."

The rationale that this population is minuscule is problematic for three reasons. First, it defies the findings of researchers (Campbell, 1989; Frieze, 1983; Russell, 1990) who argue that wife rape is a serious problem in today's society, even in small communities, and is quite possibly the most prevalent form of sexual assault. Such a rationale also contradicts research indicating that wife rape survivors make up a significant percentage of the clients at battered women's shelters—estimates of the number of shelter residents who have experienced wife rape range from 36% to 90% (Finkelhor & Yllö, 1985; personal correspondence, Laura X). Finally, arguing that wife rape survivors are insignificant in number is problematic given my findings that most service providers do not ask systematically about women's experiences of wife rape. As I indicated in Chapter 4, wife rape survivors are often hesitant to self-identify as such and/or to disclose this information without being directly asked about it. This leads me to wonder how service providers can determine the extent of this problem if they do not ask questions about it.[4]

Other reasons service providers offered for their failure to provide services to wife rape survivors are structural and include budget constraints, space limitations, and understaffing. For example, several responded,

> We cannot take on any new areas of specialization at this time.

> We have no funding to support this [outreach to marital rape survivors].

> We are not staffed to service rape victims.

Indeed, understaffing was a problem mentioned by 5% of the respondents.

Whatever the reasons, there are serious implications in the failure to provide services. As I indicated in the previous chapter, women who were denied services and shuttled from one agency to another not only felt frustrated but also were possibly endangered by this practice. Those women who were merely integrated into agencies as traditional clients felt isolated and uncomfortable because their needs as survivors of wife rape were ignored.

Given the inadequate response of service providers to wife rape survivors, we must next consider some recommendations for organizations to better meet the needs of this population.

Policy Recommendations

It is important to reiterate that the failure to claim ownership of the problem of wife rape and provide comprehensive services is not specific to the two agencies I presented in my case studies. Indeed, in failing to take responsibility for the problem of wife rape and provide comprehensive services, WASA and Refuge are representative of many other rape crisis centers and battered women's shelters in the United States (Russell, 1990; Thompson-Haas, 1987). My case studies of two organizations and analysis of the survey data suggest the need to improve services to survivors of wife rape. However, the following recommendations are shaped not only by my analysis, but also by the suggestions of wife rape survivors themselves for improving services.

Outreach

One important way to provide more assistance to survivors of wife rape is through outreach. Finkelhor and Yllö (1985) note that wife rape

has been a problem that victims have had a hard time naming, admitting, talking about, and doing something about. These obstacles can be fairly directly traced to social attitudes that have in the past minimized the problem and stigmatized its victims. (p. 187)

Providing outreach to survivors of wife rape is particularly important to legitimize the experiences of these women and provide them with the knowledge that theirs is not a personal problem. As I indicated earlier, 34% of service providers offer no specific outreach to wife rape survivors. Women's organizations are in a valuable position to provide outreach specifically to the women themselves; in doing so, they can go far to help them recognize themselves as survivors of wife rape and end the violence. To accomplish this, however, service providers must make it known that wife rape is a serious problem and that they are working to meet the needs of this population.

Agencies can begin to do this by claiming ownership of this problem and including the words *wife rape* in agency literature, brochures, and mission statements.[5] As I indicated previously, fewer than 5% of agencies provide specific brochures on wife rape. This absence of information is noticeable not only to social scientists who study organizations but, more important, to survivors of wife rape themselves. As two survivors told me,

Do you see pamphlets being held out for women who have been raped, marital raped? The only pamphlet that was put in my hand didn't have marital rape . . . they have pamphlets for date rape or stranger rape, but not for women who are raped by their husbands. They should have more information out there for women. It should be more publicized.

I think literature should be printed with rape as part of the continuum of the battering experiences. I think billboards need to focus on a combination of battering and rape by spouses to get people's attention.

Organizations can raise consciousness, not only among wife rape survivors, but also within the larger community through educational forums that address the nature of wife rape, the criminality of this type of violence, and available resources for survivors. Currently, too few service providers do this. Presentations specifically on the topic of wife rape can be offered at schools, civic association meetings, and work sites, with additional programs for social service providers. Groups that might be particularly targeted for educational programs include health care providers, law enforcement personnel, and religious advisers, all of whom are likely to come into contact with wife rape survivors and might serve as valuable resources for this population.[6]

Training Staff and Volunteers

Russell (1990) and Thompson-Haas (1987) argue that in addition to raising the consciousness of the larger community, it is also necessary to raise the consciousness of rape crisis and shelter workers. That most battered women's shelters (58%) do not train staff members and volunteers on the subject of wife rape is clearly problematic. For wife rape survivors to receive the support they need, it is essential that service providers understand the nature of this type of violence.

Service providers should be educated about the prevalence of wife rape, how to identify wife rape survivors (including a discussion of the difficulty many women have in identifying their experiences as rape), and the resources available to this population. They should also be familiar with the laws on wife rape in their state and available legal options, such as filing for restraining orders or filing criminal complaints. Service providers must also understand the trauma associated with wife rape, how the dynamics of wife rape are both similar and different from other types of violence against women, and how best to counsel wife rape survivors.[7]

Training sessions are important for workers to develop a collective representation of wife rape, as well as to convey to new members of the organization that wife rape is a serious social problem the organization has claimed responsibility for addressing. Providing information to staff members, volunteers, the larger community, and survivors of wife rape themselves is an important step service providers must take to address this problem.

Asking Sensitive Questions

One of the most important forms of outreach, neglected by rape crisis centers and battered women's shelters alike, is simply asking women routinely about wife rape. Although rape crisis and shelter workers routinely ask women about previous experiences of sexual and physical violence, fewer than half (42%) of the service providers who responded to my survey indicated that they regularly ask clients about their experiences of wife rape. Only 17% of rape crisis centers routinely ask, in contrast to 52% of battered women's shelters and 51% of combination programs. These findings are similar to those of Thompson-Haas (1987), who found that only 19% of rape crisis centers and fewer than half of battered women's shelters routinely asked about marital rape (in Russell, 1990).

As Finkelhor and Yllö (1985) note, the failure to systematically ask about wife rape may occur because

> workers in shelters are like everybody else with respect to marital rape: they have not heard a great deal about it, and since it is a highly personal subject, both difficult and embarrassing to bring up, they have often neglected to raise it. (p. 191)

This was certainly the rationale for several service providers from Refuge, who said,

> Some staff aren't comfortable with it [sexual abuse] because of personal beliefs, environment, upbringing, religion, whatever.

> I would like to be trained in this area because I would feel uncomfortable getting someone who says my husband raped me or my boyfriend raped me, you know. Maybe it's my generation.

Another staff member told me that she would feel uncomfortable asking women about wife rape because she perceived doing so as "an intrusion into their personal life."[8]

Regardless of the rationale, not asking specific questions about wife rape is problematic especially for those women who have not yet identified their experiences as wife rape or are hesitant to verbalize their experiences as rape because they are uncomfortable bringing up the subject. As Finkelhor and Yllö (1985) argue, "In the minds of many women, this perpetuate(s) the belief that marital rape is too shameful to talk about, even among workers who are familiar with family violence" (p. 191).

My interviews revealed the discomfort that many wife rape survivors feel in talking about their experiences. For example, Natalie was so uncomfortable bringing up the subject of her sexual abuse that she didn't mention it.

> I didn't know who to talk to here because I know [a staff member] does housing and so on but no one came up to me to talk about this. Thank God [the staff member] came over to me today and told me about you. I thought, this is great because, you know, I need to talk to someone because I need help, and I want to let this out and see if anyone else has been through this.

If I had not been collecting data at Refuge, it's not clear whether Natalie would have had the opportunity to talk about her experiences of sexual violence.

The most common way that service providers currently identify wife rape survivors is by encouraging women to self-identify during the intake process. This usually takes the form of asking the question, "Have you ever been raped?" This is problematic because as others (Finkelhor & Yllö, 1985; Russell, 1990) note, women are often hesitant to identify their experiences of forced sex as rape because of the myths surrounding the word *rape* in our society. Specifically, they may believe that one can be raped only by a stranger, or that it is impossible for a man to rape his wife. Not asking women specifically about their experiences of wife rape silences them. Cory described her experience: "I was at five or six shelters before this, and nobody ever asked me about the rape. Some asked me about the incest, but not about the rape. So I never brought it up." Karen, herself a survivor, said, "If you ask about their experiences [of wife rape], they'll tell you, but if you don't ask, they won't." Because many survivors of wife rape are not likely to volunteer this information, it is essential that service providers ask specific questions about this type of sexual violence.

Of those agencies who do ask specific questions about wife rape, the most common question is "Has your husband/partner ever forced you to have sex against your will?" Phrasing the question in this way rather than "Has your husband ever raped you?" is necessary and may encourage women to identify their experiences as sexual abuse. However, service providers should not stop with just one question. Instead, they should ask a variety of questions about women's sexual abuse with their partners such as "Has your partner forced the use of objects during sex? Forced you to have sex with other people? Forced you to have sex in front of others (such as children)? Forced you to look at pornography? Done things sexually that you weren't comfortable with? Pressured you to use (or not use) birth control?" and so forth.

Fewer than 6% of the service providers in this study asked a variety of questions about wife rape or provided women with a checklist to help them identify their experiences in numerous ways. Doing so might elicit a greater number of positive responses and allow women to more fully define their experiences in ways that are comfortable for them.

Equally important, systematically asking sensitive questions about wife rape is necessary to help women name their experiences and thus validate their feelings and help them to heal. As Lisa, one survivor, told me, "I feel so much better now after talking about it. . . . [I know] it's not just me—it's all starting to come together now what really happened to me, and it's not only me who went through this." Thus, asking direct questions of wife rape survivors is a fundamental way to reach out to them and a starting point for providing them with agency services.

Asking questions about wife rape is important not only for the survivors themselves, but also for service providers. Documentation of women's experiences of wife rape is an important tool for staff members to have because it provides clues about how to help these women. This point was made by two service providers at Refuge:

> You don't really know what that person is going through. You think she's acting that way because he hit her upside the head, but she's acting that way because there's really more to it than that. But she's not saying anything about [the sexual abuse], and we don't have it recorded.

> Sometimes if you say something to them [wife rape survivors], they'll open up. They won't open up themselves, but if you say it, then they'll tell you. And you really don't know how many women it's happened to because you don't ask and you don't know how to handle them.

Indeed, the identification of women as survivors of this type of violence can serve as an important tool for frontline staff in their social problems work (Loseke, 1992).

Another consideration researchers have raised is that it is important for shelter workers to know which women have been raped because raped wives are at greater risk of being killed by their partners (Browne, 1987; Campbell, 1989). This is crucial information to have so that workers can better protect the survivors of wife rape, as well as the other women in the shelter and themselves (Russell, 1980). Thus, for a variety of reasons, it is important to specifically ask sensitive questions about women's experience of wife rape.

Including the Problem of Wife Rape in the Organizational Agenda

Ultimately, in order for service providers to meet the needs of wife rape survivors they must claim ownership of this problem and actively offer a wide range of services to this population.

Shelter. A fundamental service that many survivors of wife rape require is shelter. Currently, 84% of combination battered women's shelters/rape crisis centers provide shelter to wife rape survivors. However, noticeably fewer (54%) battered women's shelters house women who have been raped by their partners.[9] Thus, one important policy recommendation is for all combination programs, battered women's shelters, and any rape crisis center that has available facilities to include these women in their target populations.

Counseling. Another necessity is to provide counseling for survivors of wife rape. As I indicated previously, many service providers offer neither individual nor group counseling to survivors of wife rape. Indeed, 98% of U.S. service providers do not provide support groups specifically for wife rape survivors, and a quarter of battered women's shelters fail to provide individual counseling to this population. Particularly problematic is that 24% of rape crisis centers either do not allow marital rape survivors into their support groups or do not have established groups that would welcome these women. It is unclear whether survivors of wife rape who contact such organizations are merely denied services or are referred elsewhere for assistance.

While they do not offer a specific support group, most service providers indicated that wife rape survivors would be welcome in other groups, such as those for battered women and survivors of sexual assault. Two thirds of the respondents indicated that they did not differentiate between wife rape and other types of violence in providing services. Indeed, the most popular responses were that these victims were welcome in other groups because the type of violence they suffered was subsumed under the heading of either domestic violence or sexual assault.

It is certainly important for wife rape survivors to be welcomed into any and all available groups. However, as I indicated in Chapter 4, it is not sufficient to treat wife rape survivors as battered women or as generic sexual assault survivors because their needs are different; wife rape survivors are often very uncomfortable in support groups for battered women or rape survivors. Thus, it is essential that specific support groups for this population not be overlooked.

Two of the women in my sample were members of a support group for wife rape survivors. Annabel and Stacey had extremely positive attitudes about this group and its role in helping them to cope with the trauma of their past experiences. For example, Annabel found the group "to be the biggest help" in healing because she could see herself in "other women's stories." Thus, designing support groups especially for survivors of wife rape is an important service for organizations to offer.

For those agencies facing staffing, budgetary, or other constraints, another option suggested by several women I interviewed was to encourage survivors of wife rape themselves to choose the type of group in which they might be most comfortable. This practice has been implemented by several service providers around the country, who responded on their surveys,

> We have domestic violence and sexual assault groups and empower women to make their own choices as to which [group] best meets their needs.

> We clearly define marital rape as part of the domestic violence spectrum as well as the rape continuum—clients are welcomed into domestic violence or rape survivors' groups, depending on what best suits their needs.

Regardless of how it is provided, counseling is a necessity. Indeed, counseling was the service that survivors of wife rape said they most needed, yet it was the service least frequently provided. For example, Terri told me, "I need more counseling, I'm real into counseling, and I like to speak to someone and have them listen to me."

Medical and legal advocacy. In addition to shelter and counseling, women's agencies can provide a variety of other services to assist wife rape survivors including medical and legal advocacy and escorts to hospitals, police departments, and courts. My survey revealed that 83% of rape crisis centers and 85% of combination programs offer these services to wife rape survivors. However, about one quarter of battered women's shelters fail to provide legal and medical advocacy to wife rape survivors. As we saw in previous chapters, wife rape survivors often meet with great resistance when they contact help providers, such as hospitals and the police. Thus, advocacy is particularly necessary.

Some Final Recommendations

Most of the women in this study would have been satisfied if a service provider had offered them shelter, counseling, and advocacy. However, several had more complex answers to the question of how agencies could best help them. For example, Karen suggested that service providers need to stop defining women's experiences for them and compartmentalizing violence against women and to begin working together. She told me,

> I don't think battered women's shelters or rape crisis centers know how to deal with it [wife rape]. They've all been so segmented, and they can't deal with it as a whole. They say we'll deal with battering and then go there for rape. These women [the victims] who've been chopped up in so many pieces can't deal with being chopped up again.
>
> I think the battered women's movement isn't for battered women, they're just into funding and trying to keep their jobs and not helping. I feel the same way about rape crisis centers—they want all the funding and only certain kinds of victims. It's amazing. . . . I think they need to cut through the bullshit and work with women. Agencies need to be flexible and deal with any dimension of the abuse. They need to deal with it from the perspective of the women.

Sally had an equally critical perspective of the current services available for survivors of wife rape. However, she suggested moving beyond the existing agencies to consider other options.

> It [wife rape] should have its own agency. If they're going to give grants out for certain things and turn you down for other things, and

if you're gonna call a rape hot line, and they tell you, "We only take
grants for this and this and you don't fit into that." And then you're
gonna call [a battered women's shelter], and they're gonna say, "We
do domestic violence and don't have education on rape." Then make
up a new program. Make a hot line, you'd get calls. You'd be
surprised, the court system would be mobbed, it really would be. If
they're gonna categorize and put us in a little hole, then make
something for us, to put it bluntly. See how many people come out
of the moldings. There'll be a heck of a lot from all walks of life.

Although both of these women targeted the lack of funding as a
significant barrier to providing adequate services, they were also
critical of the failure of women's agencies to take responsibility for
addressing the problem of wife rape.[10] Researchers such as Russell
(1990) have been equally critical of women's agencies for "becoming
preoccupied with keeping funding sources happy" (p. xxiv) and failing
to include wife rape as a major topic in their agendas.

Ultimately, most of the women in this study acknowledged that
survivors of wife rape need a variety of services, but, most important,
they need to be listened to and understood. Specifically, these women
need to have their experiences legitimized and to be included in the
agendas of women's organizations—they need to have wife rape
recognized as the serious social problem that it is.

From an organizational standpoint, my survey reveals that no one
type of organization is necessarily best to help these women. Certainly,
it is valuable that battered women's shelters and many combination
programs can provide wife rape survivors with housing and meet their
needs for safety. However, rape crisis centers are also valuable given
their expertise in dealing with sexual assault and their greater likelihood of providing medical advocacy. Currently, combination programs offer the most comprehensive services to wife rape survivors.
However, this does not necessarily lead to the conclusion that these
programs should be solely responsible for meeting the needs of this
population. Organizations vary in terms of their structure, budgetary
constraints, and missions. Furthermore, the types of agencies available
vary from one community to the next. Thus, it is impossible to argue
that any one type of organization should own this problem. Indeed, I
would argue that all three types of organizations should broaden their
missions to include wife rape in their target populations and provide
the necessary services. Most important, these service providers should

publicly claim ownership of this issue and work together to eliminate this heinous form of violence against women.

Conclusion

My goal in writing this book is to provide a better understanding of the problem of wife rape and the response of service providers. In the last two chapters, I have argued that battered women's shelters and rape crisis centers are not adequately addressing this problem. Although these findings are certainly disturbing, the lack of agency response to wife rape is not surprising if we consider Loseke's (1992) point that "social service agencies of any type are located within the larger culture. Images of problems, people, organizational design, worker activities, and sense making in various ways reflect *and* challenge or perpetuate larger cultural evaluations of problems and people" (p. 159). The inadequate response of service providers reflects the larger society's ambivalence toward the problem of wife rape and the general lack of public concern with this issue. Although we can do much to improve services to wife rape survivors and help women to end the sexual violence, this is only the first step.

The only real way to eliminate wife rape is to change the structural conditions that create and perpetuate this type of sexual violence—the inequality of men and women, husbands and wives. Wife rape is one result of male domination, both within the home and larger society. As Russell (1990) argues, the division of labor in the traditional home perpetuates wife rape; wives are economically dependent on their partners, and husbands are socially and economically powerful. Wife rape is also the consequence of a larger sexist society where violence against women is rampant and rape in marriage has traditionally been condoned.

Ultimately, the solution to the problem of wife rape is the elimination of the economic, political, and social oppression of all women (Finkelhor & Yllö, 1985; Russell, 1990). Although this should certainly be the goal of all of those working to end violence against women, such structural changes will likely be a long time in coming. However, striving to better understand the nature of wife rape and how to provide better services to this important population of women will help bring us closer to the larger goal of eliminating wife rape.

Notes

1. A common reason service providers gave for not providing such training was insufficient information on this issue. As one respondent wrote, "We touch on marital rape in training, but we don't have sufficient information to do an in-depth training." For information on training materials and how to receive more information about wife rape, please see Appendix B.

2. Of these eight, only five agencies were offering wife rape support groups when this book went to press. Most of these agencies are combined battered women's shelters/rape crisis centers. For a listing of the ones that offer wife rape support groups, please see those service providers marked with an (*) in Appendix A.

3. It should be noted that rape crisis centers were as likely as battered women's shelters to not include wife rape in their missions and to deny ownership of this issue. However, these respondents, for whatever reason, wrote fewer comments on their surveys.

4. Notably, those agencies who routinely asked about wife rape were more likely than others to estimate that this population made up a significant percentage of their clientele.

5. It is imperative that organizations try to reach specific populations such as non-English speaking women of color with regard to this issue. This may best be accomplished through the dissemination of brochures in a variety of languages, a focus on multiculturalism, and the placement of women of color in outreach offices in ethnic communities to provide direct services. The latter was done by Refuge and met with great success.

6. For recommendations on how nursing professionals can assist wife rape survivors, see Campbell and Alford (1989). Adams (1993) provides information on how religious advisers can better assist wife rape survivors.

7. Literature on how to provide training programs on the topic of wife rape is available from the Domestic Violence Project. (See Appendix B.)

8. It should be noted that only a decade ago, physical violence was considered too shameful to mention (Nicarthy, 1986).

9. Even fewer (8%) rape crisis centers provide shelter to wife rape survivors. However, this is not surprising, given that most don't have shelters or safe homes available.

10. For a rich analysis of the relationship between rape crisis centers and state funding agencies, see Matthews (1995).

Appendix A

Resource Guide for Survivors of Wife Rape

Based on my survey, the following is a listing of service providers that indicated they provide assistance to wife rape survivors. Those agencies that said they provide a support group for survivors of wife rape are indicated with an asterisk (*). The agencies are listed alphabetically by state; within each state, agencies are alphabetized by city. Most listings provide a mailing address and a telephone number. However, a few agencies did not provide a phone number.

I must stress that this guide should be used only as a basis for referrals. Organizations were included in this guide if they responded to my survey and indicated they wanted to be included on this list. Their inclusion should in no way be taken as a commentary on the quality of the services that agency provides. However, if survivors of wife rape have comments about the services they have received from these agencies, please contact me. I will forward all comments to the organizations in the hope that we can improve services to wife rape survivors.

ALABAMA

Rape Response
3600 8th Avenue South
Suite 501
Birmingham, AL 35222
(205) 323-7777 24-hour crisis

HELPline Rape Response
P.O. Box 92
Huntsville, AL 35804-0092
(205) 539-6161

Family Sunshine Center
P.O. Box 4774
Montgomery, AL 36103-4774
(334) 206-2100

ALASKA

AWAID (Abused Women's Aid in
    Crisis)
100 West 13th Avenue
Anchorage, AK 99504
(907) 279-0581 business
(907) 272-0100 crisis

Safe & Fear Free Environment
P.O. Box 94
Dillingham, AK 99576
(907) 843-2320

Emmanak Women's Shelter
P.O. Box 207
Emmanak, AK 99581
(907) 949-1434

Women in Crisis
717 9th Avenue
Fairbanks, AK 99701
(907) 452-2293

South Peninsula Women's Service,
    Inc.
3776 Lake Street, Suite 100
Homer, AK 99603
(907) 235-7712 business
(907) 235-8101 24-hour hot line

AWARE
P.O. Box 02089
Juneau, AK 99802
(907) 586-1090 crisis

Women in Safe Homes
P.O. Box 6552
Ketchikan, AK 99901-1552
(907) 225-9474

Bering Sea Women's Group
Box 1596
Nome, AK 99762
(907) 443-5491 office
1-800-570-5444 hot line

Advocates for Victims of Violence
P.O. Box 524
Valdez, AK 99686
(907) 835-2999 crisis line

ARIZONA

Crisis Center for Battered Women
401 Lexington Avenue
Fort Smith, AZ 72901
(501) 782-4596

Prehab of Arizona, Inc.
868 East University Dr.
Mesa, AZ 85203
(602) 969-4024 office
(602) 835-5555 crisis

Sojourner Center
P.O. Box 20156
Phoenix, AZ 85036
(602) 258-5348

Faith House
1535 Private Road
Prescott, AZ 86301
(602) 445-4673

Graham-Greenlee Counseling
    Center
Box 956
Safford, AZ 85548
(520) 428-4550

Tucson Rape Crisis Center
P.O. Box 40306
Tucson, AZ 85717
(520) 327-1171 business
(520) 327-7273 hot line

SAFE House
690 East 32nd St.
Yuma, AZ 85365
(602) 782-0077
(602) 782-0044

ARKANSAS

Project for Victims of Family
    Violence
P.O. Box 1923
Fayetteville, AR 72702
(501) 442-9811

Kodiak Women's Resource &
    Crisis Center
422 Millside Drive
Kodiak, AK 99615
(907) 486-6171 office
(907) 486-3625

CALIFORNIA

Rape Crisis Intervention
P.O. Box 423
Chico, CA 95927
(916) 891-1331 business
(916) 342-7273 crisis

Rape Prevention Education Program
University of California
Police Dep't. & Fire Bldg.
Kleiber Hall Drive
Davis, CA 95616-8681
(916) 752-3299

North Coast Rape Crisis Team
P.O. Box 543
Eureka, CA 95502
(707) 443-2737 business
(707) 445-2881 crisis

Kings Community Action
    Organization
1222 Lacey Boulevard
Hanford, CA 93230
Nanette Villarreal, Program
    Coordinator
(209) 582-4386

Center Against Sexual Assault
P.O. Box 2564
Hemet, CA 92546
(909) 652-8300

North County Rape Crisis & Child
   Protection Centers
P.O. Box 148
Lompoc, CA 93438
(805) 736-7273 hot line
(805) 736-8535 office

Jenesse Center, Inc.
P.O. Box 751128
Los Angeles, CA 90003
(213) 751-1145
1-800-479-7328

A Women's Place
P.O. Box 822
Castle Airport Building 265
Atwater, CA 95301
722-4357 help line
(209) 725-7900

A Safe Place to Talk
P.O. Box 1075
Oakland, CA 94604
(510) 836-2494

Women's Transitional Living Center
P.O. Box 6103
Orange, CA 92667
(714) 992-1931

YWCA-Rape Crisis Center
4161 Alma Street
Palo Alto, CA 94306
(415) 494-0993

Women Escaping a Violent
   Environment
P.O. Box 161389
Sacramento, CA 95816
(916) 448-2321

Women's Crisis Center
123 East Alisal
Salinas, CA 93901
P.O. Box 1805
Salinas, CA 93902
(408) 757-1001 24-hour hot line
(408) 757-1002 office
(408) 757-1381 fax

Calaveras Women's Crisis Center
P.O. Box 623
San Andreas, CA 95249
(209) 754-1300 office
(209) 736-4011 hot line

Family Violence Project
850 Bryant Street, Room 320
San Francisco, CA 94103
(415) 552-7550

Rape Crisis Center of San Luis
   Obispo
P.O. Box 52
San Luis Obispo, CA 93406
(805) 545-8888

Rainbow Services, Ltd.
P.O. Box 627
San Pedro, CA 90733
(310) 547-9343 Spanish/English

Shelter Services for Women
P.O. Box 3782
Santa Barbara, CA 93130
(805) 962-3778 counseling
(805) 964-5245 hot line
(805) 964-0500 Santa Barbara
   shelter

North County Rape Crisis &
  Child Protection Centers
312 East Mill, Suite 203
Santa Maria, CA 93454
(805) 928-3554 hot line
(805) 922-2994 office

YWCA of Sonoma County
  Women's Emergency Shelter
  Program
P.O. Box 7164
Santa Rosa, CA 95402
(707) 546-9922

Project Sanctuary
P.O. Box 995
Ukiah, CA 95482
(707) 482-9196 office
(707) 463-HELP (4357) hot line

Siskiyou Domestic
  Violence Program
618 4th Street
Yreka, CA 96097
(916) 842-6629

Casa de Esperanza, Inc.
P.O. Box 56
Yuba City, CA 95992-0056
(916) 674-5400 business
(916) 674-2040 crisis

COLORADO

Alternatives to Family Violence
P.O. Box 385
Commerce City, CO 80037
(303) 289-4473 administrative
(303) 289-4441 24-hour hot line
(303) 450-6161 men's program

(303) 280-0111 outclient
  women/children

Abused and Battered Humans, Inc.
P.O. Box 1050
Craig, CO 81629
(970) 824-9707 office
(970) 824-2400 24-hour hot line

Safe House Denver
Kim Cini, MSW
P.O. Box 18-0
Denver, CO 80218
(303) 836-8181 office
(303) 830-6800 hot line

Rape Intervention Team
P.O. Box 2723
Durango, CO 81302
(970) 259-3074

Crossroads Safehouse
P.O. Box 993
Fort Collins, CO 80522
(970) 482-3502 office

A Woman's Place
P.O. Box 71
Greeley, CO 80632
(970) 351-0476 office
(970) 356-4226 24-hour hot line

CONNECTICUT

Hartford YWCA Sexual Assault
  Crisis Service
135 Broad Street
Hartford, CT 06105
(203) 522-6666 24-hour hot line

YWCA/Central Connecticut Sexual
    Assault Crisis Service
169 Colony Street
Meridan, CT 06451
(203) 235-4444 office

YWCA/Central Connecticut
    Sexual Assault
169 Colony St.
Middletown, CT 06450
(203) 635-4424

Rape Crisis Center of Milford, Inc.
70 West River Street
Milford, CT 06460
(203) 878-1212 24-hour hot line

Prudence Crandall Center
P.O. Box 895
New Britain, CT 06050
(860) 225-5187 office
(860) 826-4685 hot line

YWCA of New Britain, Inc.,
    Sexual Assault Crisis Service
22 Glen Street
New Britain, CT 06051
(203) 225-4681 office
(203) 223-1787 hot line

Women's Center of Southeastern
    Connecticut
16 Jay Street
New London, CT 06320
(203) 442-4357

Susan B. Anthony Project, Inc.
434 Prospect Street
Torrington, CT 06790
(203) 489-3798 office
(203) 482-7133 crisis

Women's Emergency Shelter
P.O. Box 1503
Waterbury, CT 06721
(203) 575-0036

DISTRICT OF COLUMBIA

My Sister's Place
P.O. Box 29596
Washington, DC 20017
(202) 529-5261
(202) 529-5991 hot line

FLORIDA

Hope Family Services, Inc.
P.O. Box 1624
Bradenton, FL 34206
(841) 755-6805 crisis line
(841) 747-8499 outreach/
    counseling center

Lake Sunter Rape Crisis Center, Inc.
127 North Grove Street
Eustis, FL 32726
(904) 483-2700
1-800-330-2700

Women in Distress of Broward
    County, Inc.
P.O. Box 676
Fort Lauderdale, FL 33302
(305) 761-1133 24-hour crisis

Abuse Counseling and Treatment, Inc.
P.O. Box 60401
Fort Myers, FL 33906
(941) 939-3112

Hubbard House, Inc.
P.O. Box 4909
Jacksonville, FL 32201
(904) 399-1000

Lakeview Rape Crisis Center
1221 West Lakeview Avenue
Pensacola, FL 32501-1836
(904) 432-1222, ext. 302 main
    switchboard
(904) 433-7273 crisis line

Center for Abuse and Rape
    Emergencies (CARE)
P.O. Box 234
Punta Gorda, FL 33951-0234
(941) 627-6000 hot line
(941) 479-6465 hot line
(941) 639-5499 business

The Spring of Tampa Bay, Inc.
P.O. Box 4772
Tampa, FL 33677-4771

ILLINOIS

Mutual Grand, Inc.
P.O. Box 843
Aurora, IL 60507

Rape Crisis Center of
    Mid-Central Illinois
P.O. Box 995
Bloomington, IL 61702-0995
(309) 828-1022 office

The Women's Center
406 West Mill Street
Carbondale, IL 62901
(618) 549-4807

Safe Passage
P.O. Box 621
DeKalb, IL 60115
(815) 756-5228 hot line
(815) 756-7930 office

Life Span
P.O. Box 445
Des Plaines, IL 60016
(708) 824-0382 office
(708) 824-4454 24-hour hot line

Volunteers of America, Illinois
40700 State Street, Suite 2
East St. Louis, IL 62205
(618) 271-9833

Call for Help, Inc.-Sexual Assault
    Victim's Care Unit
9400 Lebanon Road
Edgemont, IL 62203
(618) 397-0975
(618) 394-2903

Community Crisis Center
P.O. Box 1390
Elgin, IL 60121
(708) 697-2380

YWCA
DuPae District
739 Roosevelt Road, Suite 8-210
Glen Ellyn, IL 60137
(708) 790-6600 office
(708) 971-3927 hot line

Family Shelter Service
P.O. Box 3404
Glen Ellyn, IL 60138
(708) 469-5650

Anna Bixby Women's Center
213 South Shaw Street
Harrisburg, IL 62946
1-800-421-8456 hot line
(618) 252-8389 hot line

South Suburban Family Shelter, Inc.
P.O. Box 937
Homewood, IL 60430
(708) 335-4125 office
(708) 335-3028 24-hour hot line

YWCA Sexual Assault Program
412 1st Avenue
Sterling, IL 61081
(815) 629-0333
(815) 626-7277 hot line

Constance Morris House
c/o 6125 South Archer Road
Summet, IL 60501
(708) 485-5254 crisis

Sexual Assault & Family
   Emergencies
P.O. Box 192
Vandalia, IL 62471
(618) 283-1414

INDIANA

Women's Alternatives, Inc.
P.O. Box 1302
Anderson, IN 46013
(317) 643-0200

Family Crisis Shelter
P.O. Box 254
Crawfordsville, IN 47933
(317) 362-2030

YWCA Battered Women's Shelter
118 Vine Street
Evansville, IN 47708
(812) 422-1191

YWCA Shelter for Women
   Victims of Violence
P.O. Box 11242
Fort Wayne, IN 46856-1242
(219) 447-7233 office
1-800-441-4073 hot line

YWCA Family Intervention
   Center
406 East Sycamore
Kokomo, IN 46901
(317) 459-0314

YWCA-Domestic Violence
   Intervention & Prevention
   Program
605 North 6th Street
Lafayette, IN 47901
(317) 423-1118 24-hour hot line

The Shelter, Inc.
P.O. Box 894
Lawrenceburg, IN 38464

Women's Services, A Division of
   Family Service Society, Inc.
428 South Washington Street, Suite
   327
Marion, IN 46953
(317) 662-9971 business
(317) 664-0701 hot line

Council on Domestic Abuse
P.O. Box 392
Terre Haute, IN 47808
(812) 232-1736

IOWA

ACCESS (Assault Care Center
    Extending Shelter and Support)
P.O. Box 1965
Ames, IA 50010
(515) 232-2303 hot line
(515) 232-5418 office

YWCA Shelter for Battered Women
2410 Mount Pleasant
Burlington, IA 52601
(319) 752-0606 office
(319) 752-4475 hot line

YWCA Critical Services Sexual
    Assault Intervention Program
    & Domestic Violence Program
    & Shelter
318 5th Street, Southeast
Cedar Rapids, IA
(319) 365-1458 YWCA
(319) 363-5490 sexual assault crisis
    hot line
(319) 363-2093 domestic violence
    hot line

YWCA Women's Resource Center
317 7th Avenue South
Clinton, IA 52732
(319) 242-2118 business
(319) 243-STOP crisis

Children & Families of Iowa
1111 University Avenue
Des Moines, IA 50314
(515) 288-1981
Family Violence Center
(515) 243-6147

Domestic/Sexual Assault Outreach
    Center
P.O. Box 173
Fort Dodge, IA 50501
(515) 955-2273

Rape Victim Advocacy Program
17 West Prentiss Street
Iowa City, IA 52240
(310) 335-6001 office
(310) 335-6000 hot line
1-800-284-7821 hot line

Sexual Assault & Domestic Abuse
    Advocacy Program
119 Sycamore, Suite 100
Muscatine, IA 52761
(319) 263-8080

CASADV
Box 1565
Sioux City, IA
(712) 258-7233

KANSAS

Crisis Center of Dodge City, Inc.
P.O. Box 1173
Dodge City, KS 67801
(316) 225-6987

The Crisis Center, Inc.
P.O. Box 1526
Manhattan, KS 66505
(913) 539-7935 business
1-800-727-2785 24-hour hot line

Northwest Kansas Family Shelter
P.O. Box 284
Hays, KS 67601
(913) 625-4202

Safehouse, Inc.
101 East 4th Street
National Bank Building, Suite 214
Pittsburgh, KS 66762
(316) 231-8251
1-800-794-9148 hot line

YWCA Women's Crisis
    Center/Safehouse
420 East English, Suite B
Wichita, KS 67202
(312) 267-7233

Cowley County Safe Homes, Inc.
P.O. Box 181
Winfield, KS 67156
(316) 221-7300 office
(316) 221-HELP
1-800-794-7672

KENTUCKY

Pathways Rape Victim Services
    Program
201 22nd Street
Ashland, KY 41101
(606) 324-1141
1-800-562-8909

Safe Harbor of Northeast Kentucky,
    Inc.
P.O. Box 2163
Ashland, KY 41105-2163
(606) 325-5138

The Rape Crisis and Prevention
    Center
P.O. Box 1854
Bowling Green, KY 42101-1854
(502) 782-5014

(502) 782-5017
1-800-347-1848 crisis

Sanctuary, Inc.
P.O. Box 1265
Hopkinsville, KY 42240
1-800-766-0000
(502) 885-4572

OASIS
P.O. Box 1325
Owensboro, KY

Purchase Area Spouse Abuse Center
P.O. Box 98
Paducah, KY 42002-0098
(502) 443-6001

LKLP Safe House
HC 32, Box 2150
Redfox, KY 41847
(606) 439-1552 business
(606) 439-5129 crisis
1-800-928-3131 crisis

Bethany House Spouse Abuse
    Shelter
Box 864
Somerset, KY 42502
(606) 679-8852 crisis
1-800-755-2017

LOUISIANA

Family Counseling Agency
P.O. Box 1908
Alexandria, LA 71309
(318) 448-0284

Chez Hope, Inc.
P.O. Box 98
Franklin, LA 70538
1-800-331-5303

Safety Net for Abused Persons
    (SNAP)
P.O. Box 10207
New Abiva, LA 70562-0207
(318) 367-7627

Contact Peninsula, Inc.
P.O. Box
Newport Hills, LA 32601

MAINE

Abused Women's Advocacy Project
P.O. Box 713
Auburn, ME 04212
(207) 795-4020
1-800-559-2927 in-state

The Family Violence Project
P.O. Box 304
Augusta, ME 04332
(207) 623-8637 business
(207) 623-3569 crisis

Spruce Run Association
P.O. Box 653
Bangor, ME 04402-0653
(207) 945-5102
(207) 947-0496 24-hour hot line
Collect calls accepted

A Sexual Assault Helpline
P.O. Box 1018
Caribou, ME 04736
1-800-559-3304

(207) 762-4851

Womancare/Aegis Association
P.O. Box 192
Dover-Foxcroft, ME 04426
(207) 564-8165 daytime
(207) 564-8401 after hours

Sexual Assault Victims
    Emergency Services
P.O. Box 349
Farmington, ME 04938
(207) 778-9522 office
1-800-221-9191 hot line

Womankind, Inc.
P.O. Box 493
Machias, ME 04654
(207) 255-3031 office
(207) 255-4785 hot line
1-800-432-7303

Rape Crisis Center, Inc.
P.O. Box 1371
Portland, ME 04104
(207) 774-3613

MARYLAND

Sexual Assault/Domestic Violence
    Center, Inc.
6229 North Charles Street
Baltimore, MD 21212
(410) 377-8111 office
(410) 828-6390 hot line

Sexual Assault Center
Prince George's Hospital Center
3001 Hospital Drive
Cheverly, MD 20785
(301) 618-3154 hot line and office

Heartly House, Inc.
P.O. Box 857
Frederick, MD 21705-0831

*Abused Persons Program
Calvert County Health Department
P.O. Box 980
Prince Frederick, MD 20678
(301) 855-1075 hot line
(410) 535-1121 hot line

Life Crisis Center
P.O. Box 387
Salisbury, MD 21803-0387
(410) 749-4363
(410) 749-0632

Family and Children's Services
Domestic Violence Program of
    Carrol County
22 North Court Street
Westminster, MD 21157
(410) 876-1233 office
(410) 857-0077 hot line
(410) 876-4791 fax

MASSACHUSETTS

Transition House
P.O. Box 530
Harvard Square Station
Cambridge, MA
(617) 661-7203 hot line

Battered Women's Resources, Inc.
P.O. Box 2503
Fitchburg, MA 01420
(508) 342-9355
(508) 630-1031

(508) 368-1311
(508) 342-2919

Cape Cod Rape Crisis Center
160 Bassett Lane
Hyannis, MA 02601
(508) 771-6507
1-800-439-6507

Rape Crisis Services of Greater
    Lowell
70 Industrial Avenue East
Lowell, MA 01852
1-800-542-5212 office
(508) 452-7721 hot line

Women's Services Center
    of West Massachusetts
146 First Street
Pittsfield, MA 01201
(413) 499-2425
(413) 433-0089
(413) 663-9709 (North)
(413) 528-2320 (South)

Abby's House
21-23 Crown Street
Worcester, MA 01609
(508) 756-5486

MICHIGAN

Women's Information
    Service, Inc.
P.O. Box 1074
Big Rapids, MI 49307
(616) 796-6692 business
(616) 796-6600 24-hour crisis
1-800-374-WISE

Safe Shelter, Inc.
275 Pipestone
Benton Harbor, MI 49022
(616) 983-4275 hot line
(616) 925-2280 office

YWCA
25 Sheldon Southeast
Grand Rapids, MI 49503
(616) 459-4652 shelter
(616)-459-4681 main line

LACASA/SARA
P.O. Box 72
Howell, MI 48844
(517) 548-1352 LACASA
    domestic violence
(517) 548-4228 SARA
    rape crisis center
(517) 548-3034 fax

Aware, Inc.
P.O. Box 1526
Jackson, MI 49204
(517) 783-2861

Council on Domestic Violence &
    Sexual Assault
P.O. Box 2289
Midland, MI 48641
(517) 835-6771

Women's Aid Service, Inc.
P.O. Box 743
Mount Pleasant, MI 48804-0743
(517) 772-9168 hotline
(517) 539-1046 hotline
(517) 463-6014 hotline
(517) 773-0078

Women's Resource Center of
    Northern Michigan, Inc.
423 Porter
Petoskey, MI 49770
(616) 347-0082 24-hour hot line
(616) 347-0067 main office
(616) 347-1572 domestic abuse

Family Crisis Center
P.O. Box 1158
Polson, MT 59860
(406) 883-3350-hot line
1-800-228-1038-hot line

HAVEN
P.O. Box 787
Pontiac, MI 48343
(810) 334-1284 business
(810) 334-1274 24-hour hot line

Underground Railroad
P.O. Box 565
Saginaw, MI 48606
(517) 755-0411 main line

Eastern Upper Peninsula (EUP)
    Domestic Violence Program
P.O. Box 636
Sault Sainte Marie, MI 49783
(906) 635-0566
1-800-882-1515

MINNESOTA

Listening Ear Crisis Center
418 3rd Avenue East, No. 2
Alexandria, MN 56308
1-800-854-9001

Austin Medical Center-Victims
   Crisis Center
101 14th Street, Northwest
Austin, MN 55912
(507) 437-6680
Austin Medical Office main office
2100 Pillsbury Ave.
South Minneapolis, MN 55404
(507) 433-7351

Sexual Violence Center of Carver
   and Scott Counties
510 Chestnut Street North, Suite
   204
Chaska, MN 55318
(612) 448-5425 hot line
(612) 871-5100 office

Hands of Hope Resource Center
P.O. Box 67
Little Falls, MN 56349
(612) 632-1657

CADA
P.O. Box 466
Mankato, MN 56002
(507) 625-8688 office
(507) 625-7233 hot line
1 800 477-0466

New Horizons Crisis Center
1104 East College Drive
P.O. Box 51
Marshall, MN 56258
(507) 532-5764 main line

Harriet Tubman Center
Room 318 City Hall
350 South 5th Street
Minneapolis, MN 55415

(612) 673-2244 legal office
(610) 825-0000 crisis

Sexual Violence Program
University of Minnesota
253 Nicholson Hall
216 Pillsbury Drive, Southeast
Minneapolis, MN 55455
(612) 625-6512 business
(612) 626-1300 hot line

Women's Resource Center
   of Steele County
125 W. Front St.
Owatonna, MN 55060
(507) 451-1202 office
1-800-451-1202

Central Minnesota Sexual Assault
   Center
601 1/2 Mall Germain, Suite 204
St. Cloud, MN 56301
(320) 251-4357 (HELP)
1-800-237-5090

Central Minnesota Task Force
   on Battered Women
P.O. Box 195
St. Cloud, MN 56302
(612) 253-6900 office
(612) 251-7203 St. Cloud
   intervention project
(612) 252-1603 hot line

Sexual Offense Services
   of Ramsey County
1619 Dayton Avenue, #201
St. Paul, MN 55104
(612) 298-5898 main number

Violence Intervention Project
P.O. Box 96
Thief River Falls, MN 56701
(218) 681-5557 office
1-800-660-6667 (valid only in
    northwest Minnesota)

Sexual Assault Program of
    Northern St. Louis County
505 12th Avenue, West
Virginia, MN 55792
(218) 749-4725 main number

Woodland Center
    Shelter House
P.O. Box 787
Willmar, MN 56201
1-800-476-3234 (valid only in
    Minnesota)
(320) 231-9154 shelter house

Women's Resource Center
77 East 5th St.
Winona, MN 55987
(507) 452-4440 main number

MISSISSIPPI

Sexual Assault Crisis Center
P.O. Box 10016
Hattiesburg, MS 39406
(601) 264-7078 business
(601) 264-7777 crisis

Catholic Charities
    Rape Crisis Center
P.O. Box 2248
Jackson, MS 39225
(601) 982-RAPE (7273) crisis
(601) 366-3880 crisis

MISSOURI

Hope House, Inc.
P.O. Box 520409
Independence, MO 64052
(816) 461-HOPE hot line

Jefferson City Rape &
    Abuse Crisis Service
Box 416
Jefferson City, MO 65102
(573) 634-8346 office
(573) 634-4911 hot line
1-800-303-0013 24 hours

Lafayette House
P.O. Box 1765
Joplin, MO 64804
1-800-416-1772 office

Harbor Lights
P.O. Box 398
Kimberling City, MO 65686
(417) 739-2118
1-800-831-6863 24-hour hot line

Haven House, Inc.
P.O. Box 4875
Poplar Bluff, MO 63902
(314) 686-4873 crisis line

ALIVE (Alternatives to Living in
    Violent Environments)
P.O. Box 11201
St. Louis, MO 63105
(314) 993-2777

St. Martha's Hall
P.O. Box 4950
St. Louis, MO 63108

(314) 533-1313 office/hot line

Victim Service Council
7900 Carondelet, 4th floor
St. Louis, MO 63105
(314) 889-3075 office/crisis

Women's Self-Help Center
2838 Olive
St. Louis, MO 63103
(314) 531-9100 business
(314) 531-2003 crisis

The Center for Women &
  Children Survival
  Adult Abuse, Inc.
137 East Culton
P.O. Box 344
Warrensburg, MO 64093
(816) 429-1088 hotline
(816) 429-2847 office

MONTANA

Violence Free Crisis Line
P.O. Box 1385
Kalispell, MT 59903-1385

Women's Place
501 West Alder
Missoula, MT 59802

NEBRASKA

CISDA
1211 Main
Crete, NE 68333
(402) 826-2332

The Crisis Center for Domestic
  Abuse & Sexual Assault
P.O. Box 622
Fremont, NE 68025
(402) 721-4340 crisis
1-800-876-6238

Family Rescue Services
107 East 2nd
Gordon, NE 69343
(308) 282-0126 Gordon hot line
(302) 432-4113 Chadron hot line

Crisis Center
P.O. Box 1008
2121 North Webb Road
Grand Island, NE 68802
(308) 382-8250 business
(308) 381-0555 24-hour hot line

Parent-Child Center
P.O. Box 722
513 North Grant, No. 11
Lexington, NE 68850-0722
(308) 324-2336 office
(308) 324-3040 hot line
1-800-215-3040 crisis line

Nebraska Domestic Violence
Sexual Assault Coalition
315 South 9th Street, No. 18
Lincoln, NE 68508-2253
(402) 476-6256

Domestic Abuse/Sexual Assault
  Services
P.O. Box 714
McCook, NE 69001
(308) 345-5534 crisis
Collect calls accepted

Sandhills Crisis Intervention
    Program
P.O. Box 22
Ogllala, NE 69153
(308) 284-8477 office
(308) 284-6055 24-hour crisis hot
    line

The Shelter
Box 4346
Omaha, NE 68104
(402) 558-5708

YWCA
222 South 29th Street
Omaha, NE 68131
(402) 345-6555 office
(402) 345-7273 crisis

Domestic Violence Emergency
    Services Task Force
P.O. Box 434
Scottsbluff, NE 69363-0434
(308) 436-4357 hot line

NEVADA

Committee Against Domestic
    Violence
Box 2531
Elko, NV 89803
(702) 738-6524 office
(702) 738-9454 hot line

Support Inc. Family Crisis Center
P.O. Box 583
Ely, NV 89301
(702) 289-2270 office and hot line
    during business hrs

(702) 289-8808 hot line after
    business hrs. Local sheriff will
    page support volunteer during
    non-business hrs.

Temporary Assistance for Domestic
    Crisis
P.O. Box 43264
Las Vegas, NV 89116
(702) 646-4981 24-hour hot line
(702) 368-1533 office

Support Inc. Family Crisis Center
P.O. Box 485
Pioche, NV 89043
(702) 962-5888
289-2294 fax

NEW HAMPSHIRE

Family Health Services/Response to
    Sexual & Domestic Violence
54 Willow Street
Berlin, NH 03570
(603) 752-2040 office
1-800-852-3388 crisis
(603) 752-5674 response office

YWCA Crisis Service
72 Concord Street
Manchester, NH 03101
(603) 625-5785 office
(603) 668-2299 24-hour hot line

Rape & Assault Support
    Services, Inc.
P.O. Box 217
Nashua, NH 03061
(603) 883-3044 24-hour hot line

Sexual Assault Support Services
7 Junkins Avenue
Portsmouth, NH 03801
(603) 436-4107 office
(603) 436-1627 hot line
1-800-747-7070 hot line

NEW JERSEY

SOLACE
P.O. Box 1309
Blackwood, NJ 08102
(609) 227-1234 24-hour crisis

People Against Spouse Abuse
P.O. Box 755
Glassboro, NJ 08028
(609) 881-3335 hot line
(609) 848-5557 hot line

YWCA of Bergen County
    Rape Crisis Center
285 Passaic Street
Hackensack, NJ
(201) 487-2227 hot line
(201) 488-7110 office

Women's Center of Monmouth
    County
Bethany Commons, Bldg. 3
1 Bethany Road
Hazlet, NJ 07730
(908) 264-4111

Sexual Assault Support Services-
    Emergency Room
St. Barnabas Medical Center
Old Short Hills Road
Livingston, NJ 07039
(201) 533-5180 main #

Roosevelt Hospital RCIC
P.O. Box 151
Metuchen, NJ 08840
(908) 321-6800

Atlantic County Women's Center
P.O. Box 311
Northfield, NJ 08225
(609) 646-6767 office
1-800-286-4184 hot line

Salem County Women's Services
P.O. Box 125
Salem, NJ 08079
(609) 935-6655 hot line
(609) 935-8012 office

Somerset Rape Crisis Service
95 Veterans Memorial Drive
Somerville, NJ 08876

YWCA of Trenton
140 East Hanover Street
Trenton, NJ 08608
(609) 989-9592 office
(609) 989-9332 rape crisis hot line
(609) 396-8291 YWCA main #

Union County Rape Crisis Center
300 North Avenue, East
Westfield, NJ 07090
(908) 233-7273 main #

NEW MEXICO

Albuquerque Rape Crisis Center
1025 Mariposa, Southeast
Albuquerque, NM 87108
(505) 266-7711 main #

The Shelter for Victims
  of Domestic Violence
P.O. Box 1732
Clovis, NM 88101
(505) 762-7853 office
1-800-401-0305 hot line

Laguna Family Services
P.O. Box 194
Laguna, NM 87026
(505) 552-9702 office
1-800-530-2199 hot line

LaCasa, Inc.
P.O. Box 2463
Las Cruces, NM 88004
(505) 526-9513 crisis line
1-800-376-2272 crisis
(505) 526-2819 office

Roswell Refuge for Battered Adults
P.O. Box 184
Roswell, NM 88202-0184
(505) 624-0666 main #

Santa Fe Rape Crisis Center, Inc.
P.O. Box 16346
Santa Fe, NM 87506
(505) 986-9111 main #

NEW YORK

Albany County Rape Crisis Center
112 State Street, Room 1100
Albany, NY 12207
(518) 447-7100 office
(518) 445-7547 24-hour hot line

Cayuga Counseling Services Inc/
  Sexual Assault Victims
  Advocate Resource
27 East Genesee
Auburn, NY 13021
(315) 253-9795 office
(315) 252-2112 24-hour hot line

Crime Victims Assistance Center,
  Inc.
P.O. Box 836
Binghamton, NY 13902
(607) 723-3200 office
(607) 722-4256 crisis

Park Slope Safe Homes Project
P.O. Box 15429
Van Brunt Station
Brooklyn, NY 11215
(718) 499-2151 hot line
(718) 788-6947 office

Rape Crisis Intervention
Victims of Violence Program
The Long Island College Hospital
340 Henry Street, 6th floor
Brooklyn, NY 11201
(718) 780-1459 hot line
(718) 780-4632 office
(718) 780-1912 office

Rape Crisis Center
Washington County
Mary McClellan Hospital
Cambridge, NY 12816
(518) 677-3019 office
1-800-225-7114

St. Lawrence Valley Renewal
    House for Victims of
    Family Violence, Inc.
39 Main Street
Canton, NY 13617
(315) 379-9845 office
(315) 265-2422 24-hour hot line

Victims Information Bureau of
    Suffolk
P.O. Box 5483
Hauppauge, NY 11788
(516) 360-3606 hot line
(516) 360-3730 office

The Putaam Northern Westchester
    Women's Resource Center
2 Mahopac Plaza
Mahopac, NY 10541
(914) 628-2166 hot line
(914) 628-9284 office

Family & Children's Service
826 Chilton Avenue
Niagara Falls, NY 14301
(716) 285-6984 main #

Niagara County Rape Crisis Services
775 Third Street
Niagara Falls, NY 14302
(716) 285-3518 hot line
(716) 278-1825 office

YWCA of the Tonawandas
49 Tremont Street
North Tonawanda, NY 14120
(716) 692-5580 office
(716) 692-5643 hot line

Victims of Violence
Liberty Resources, Inc.
218 Liberty Street
Oneida, NY 13421
(315) 363-3404 office
(315) 366-5060 hot line

Alternatives for Battered Women,
    Inc.
P.O. Box 14604
Rochester, NY 14604
(716) 232-7353 hot line
(716) 232-5200 office

Cattaraugus Community
    Action, Inc.
P.O. Box 308
25 Jefferson Street
Salamanca, NY 14779
(716) 945-1041 office
(716) 945-3970 hot line

Saratoga Domestic Services & Rape
    Crisis
480 Broadway LL 20
Saratoga Springs, NY 12866
(518) 583-0280 office
(518) 584-8188 hot line

Rape Crisis Service of Planned
    Parenthood
414 Union Street
Schenectady, NY 12305
(518) 346-2266 hot line/rape crisis
(518) 374-5353 office/planned
    parenthood

YWCA of Schenectady
44 Washington Avenue
Schenectady, NY 12305
(518) 374-3386 hot line
(518) 374-3386 office

Dorthy Day House
P.O. Box 77
Syracuse, NY 13205
(315) 474-7011 hot line

Rape Crisis Program for Rensselaer
    County
2215 Burdett Avenue
Troy, NY 12180
(518) 271-3445 office
(518) 271-3257 hot line

Unity House Families in Crisis
    Program
3215 6th Avenue
Troy, NY 12180
(518) 272-2370

YWCA Rape Crisis Services
1000 Cornelia Street
Utica, NY 13502
(315) 797-7740 hot line Utica
    County
(315) 866-4120 Herkimer County
    Rape Crisis
(315) 733-0665 hot line

St. Joseph's Medical Center
    Program on Family Violence
53 South Broadway, 2nd Floor
Yonkers, NY 10701
(914) 966-6339 main #

NORTH CAROLINA

Family Crisis Center
P.O. Box 2161
Asheboro, NC 27204
(910) 629-4159 main #

Rape Crisis Center, Inc.
P.O. Box 7453
Asheville, NC 28802
(704) 252-0562 business
(704) 255-7576 crisis

Rape Crisis Alliance of Alamance
    County, Inc.
P.O. Box 673
Burlington, NC 27216
(910) 228-0813 office
(910) 228-0364 24-hour crisis

United Family Service Shelter for
    Battered Women
P.O. Box 220312
Charlotte, NC 28222
(704) 332-2513

Rape Crisis of Durham
331 West Main Street, Suite 304
Durham, NC 27713
(919) 688-4457

Albemarle Hopeline
P.O. Box 2064
Elizabeth City, NC 27906-2064
(919) 338-3011 hot line
(919) 338-5338 office

Pitt County Family Violence
    Program d/b/a/ New Directions
P.O. Box 8429

Greenville, NC 27835
(919) 752-3811

The Healing Place
722 5th Avenue, West
Hendersonville, NC 28793
(704) 692-0495 main #

Family Guidance Center/First Step
    Domestic Violence Services
No. 17 Highway 70 Southeast
Hickory, NC 28602
(704) 322-1400 main #

Onslow Women's Center
P.O. Box 1622
Jacksonville, NC 28541
(910) 347-4000 office & crisis

Shelter Home of Caldwell County,
    Inc.
P.O. Box 426
Lenoir, NC 28645
(704) 758-0888 main #

Reach, Inc.
P.O. Box 977
Murphy, NC 28906
(704) 837-8064 main #

Interact
P.O. Box 11096
Raleigh, NC 27604
(919) 828-7740 domestic
(919) 828-3005 sexual assault
(919) 828-7501 office

Family Crisis Council
131 West Council Street
Salisbury, NC 28144
(704) 636-4718 main #

Haven (Helping Abuse and
    Violence End Now) in Lee
    County
223 Carthage Street
P.O. Box 3191
Sanford, NC 27330
(919) 774-8923 main #

Cleveland County Abuse
    Prevention Council, Inc.
P.O. Box 2895
Shelby, NC 28151
(704) 487-9325 office
(704) 481-0043 crisis

Rape Crisis Center, Inc.
P.O. Box 7453
50 S. French Broad Ave.
Asheville, NC 28802
(704) 255-7576 office
(704) 252-0562 crisis

Options to Domestic Violence/
    Sexual Assault, Inc.
P.O. Box 1387
Washington, NC 27889
(919) 946-3219 main #

REACH of Haywood County
P.O. Box 206
Waynesville, NC 28786
(704) 456-7898 main #

My Sister's House
1400 Fifth Street
Statesville, NC 28677
(704) 872-3405 crisis

Safe, Inc.
P.O. Box 445
Wilkesboro, NC 28697
(910) 667-7656

Domestic Violence Shelter &
   Services, Inc.
P.O. Box 1555
Wilmington, NC 28402
(910) 343-0703

Family Services, Inc.
610 Coliseum Drive
Winston-Salem, NC 27106
(910) 723-8125 24-hour
   domestic violence hot line
(910) 722-4457 24-hour sexual
   assault hot line

NORTH DAKOTA

Abused Adult Resource Center
Box 167
Bismarck, ND 58502
(701) 222-8370

Domestic Violence & Rape Crisis
   Center
Box 1081
Dickinson, ND 58602-1081
(701) 225-4506

Abuse & Rape Crisis Center
111 South 4th Street
Grand Forks, ND 58201
(701) 746-0405 office
(701) 746-8900 crisis

Abuse Resource Network
Box 919
Lisbon, ND 58054-0919
(701) 683-5061

Domestic Violence Crisis Center
P.O. Box 881
Minot, ND 58702

(701) 852-2258 office
(701) 857-2200 crisis

McLean Family Resource Center
P.O. Box 506
Washburn, ND 58577
(701) 462-8643

OHIO

Alliance Area Domestic
   Violence Shelter
P.O. Box 3622
Alliance, OH 44601
(216) 823-7223 main #

My Sister's Place
P.O. Box 1158
Athens, OH 45701
(614) 593-3402
1-800-443-3402

YWCA House of Peace
Shelter for Battered Women
P.O. Box 26
Batavia, OH 45103
(513) 753-7281 domestic violence
1-800-644-4460 rape

American Red Cross
   Rape Crisis Services
2213 Cleveland Ave., NW
Canton, OH 44709
(216) 452-1111 hot line

Domestic Violence Project, Inc.
P.O. Box 9432
Canton, OH 44711-9432
(216) 453-SAFE
(216) 588-COPE

Women Safe
P.O. Box 656
Chardon, OH 44024
(216) 564-9555 crisis

Women Helping Women, Inc.
216 East 9th Street
Cincinnati, OH 45202
(513) 381-6003

First Step
P.O. Box 1103
Fastoria, OH 44830
(419) 435-7300 business
1-800-466-6228 crisis

Open Arms Domestic Violence
    Shelter & Rape Crisis Services
P.O. Box 496
Findlay, OH 45839
(419) 422-4766 crisis

Dave House Protective Shelter
c/o 244 Dayton Street
Hamilton, OH 45011
(513) 863-7099

Community Assault Prevention
    Services of Gallia
Jackson & Meigs Counties
P.O. Box 207
19 Harding Avenue
Jackson, OH 45640
(614) 286-6611
(614) 286-6433

Crossroads Crisis Center, Inc.
P.O. Box 643
Lima, OH 45802
(419) 228-HELP hot line
(419) 228-6692 business

The Domestic Violence Shelter
P.O. Box 1524
Mansfield, OH 44901
(419) 774-5840
1-800-931-SAFE

Eve, Inc.
P.O. Box 122
Marietta, OH 45750
(614) 374-5819 main #

Turning Point
P.O. Box 822
Marion, OH 43302
(614) 382-8988
1-800-232-6505 (Ohio only)

New Directions
Box 453
Mount Vernon, OH 43050
(614) 397-4357 main #

Project Women
1316 East High Street
Springfield, OH 45505
(513) 325-3707 office
1-800-634-9893

YWCA Rape Crisis Center
1018 Jefferson Avenue
Toledo, OH 43624
(419) 241-7006 office
(419) 241-7273 hot line

Rape Crisis Team of Trumbull
    County
P.O. Box 1743
Warren, OH 44482
(216) 394-4060
(216) 393-1565 contact

Someplace SAFE, Inc.
P.O. Box 282
Warren, OH 44482
(330) 393-3003 office
(330) 393-3004 fax
(330) 393-1565

Greene County Domestic Violence
    Project, Inc.
Box 271
Xenia, OH 45385
(513) 372-4552 24-hr hot line
(513) 426-2334 Fairborne 24-hour
    hot line
(513) 376-8526 office

Family Service Agency Rape Info &
    Counseling
535 Marmion Avenue
Youngstown, OH 44502
(216) 782-5664

OKLAHOMA

ACMI House
P.O. Box 397
Altus, OK 73522
(405) 482-3800 24-hr hot line
1-800-466-3805
(405) 482-7449 office

Women's Service & Family
    Resource Center
P.O. Box 1539
Chickasha, OK 73023
(405) 222-1818 crisis
(405) 224-8256 office

Action Associates, Inc.
P.O. Box 1534
Clinton, OK 73601
(405) 323-2604 hot line
(405) 323-0838 hot line

YWCA Crisis Center
525 South Quincy
Enid, OK 73702
(405) 234-7644 24-hour hot line
Collect calls accepted

Stillwater Domestic Violence
    Services, Inc.
P.O. Box 1059
Stillwater, OK 74076
(405) 377-2344 office
(405) 624-3020 crisis

Domestic Violence Intervention
    Services, Inc.
1419 East 15th Street
Tulsa, OK 74120
(918) 585-3163 business
(918) 585-3143 24-hour hot line

OREGON

May Day Incorporated
18 21st Street, #12
Baker City, OR 97814
(503) 523-4134

Central Oregon Battering & Rape
    Alliance (COBRA)
P.O. Box 1086
Bend, OR 97709
(503) 382-9227 office
1-800-356-2369 hot line

Rape Crisis Center, Inc.
P.O. Box 73
Hillsboro, OR 97123
(503) 640-5311 hot line

Women's Violence
    Intervention Program
P.O. Box 426
Lincoln City, OR 97367
(541) 994-5959 main #

Hendemer House Family
    Crisis Shelter
P.O. Box 26
McMinnville, OR 97128
(503) 472-1503 hot line
(503) 472-0244 hot line

Helping Hands
P.O. Box 441
Hood River, OR 97031

Coos County Women's Crisis
    Service
P.O. Box 791
North Bend, OR 97459
(503) 756-7000 hot line
(503) 756-7864 office

Project DOVE (Domestic
    Violence Eliminated)
P.O. Box 745
Ontario, OR 97914
(503) 889-6316 office
(503) 889-2000 crisis

Domestic Violence Services
P.O. Box 152
Pendleton, OR 97801
(503) 278-0241 hot line
1-800-833-1161 crisis line
(503) 276-3322 office

Portland Women's Crisis Line
P.O. Box 42610
Portland, OR 97242
(503) 232-9751 office
(503) 235-5333 crisis

Mid-Valley Women's Crisis Center
P.O. Box 851
Salem, OR 97308
(503) 399-7722 hot line
(503) 378-1572 office

Women's Crisis Center
P.O. Box 187
Tillamook, OR 97141
(503) 842-9486 main #

PENNSYLVANIA

Crime Victims Council
    of the Lehigh Valley
509 North 7th Street
Allentown, PA 18102
(610) 437-6610 office
(610) 437-6611 24-hour hot line

Turning Point of Lehigh Valley
c/o E. Kleppinger
P.O. Box 5355
Bethlehem, PA 18015
(610) 867-6477

McKean County Victims'
    Resource Center
24 West Corydon Street
Bradford, PA 16701
(814) 368-4235 office
(814) 368-6325 24-hour hot line

Crime Victim Services
222 West Cunningham Street
Butler, PA 16001
(412) 282-7273

Women in Need/Victim Services
P.O. Box 25
Chambersburg, PA 17201
(717) 264-4444
1-800-621-6660

Stop Abuse For Everyone
P.O. Box 108
Clarion, PA 16214
1-800-992-3039
(814) 226-8481

The Rape Crisis Center, Inc.
1064 B East Main Street
Clarion, PA 16214
(814) 226-7273

Clearfield County Rape Crisis
    Center
P.O. Box 248
Clearfield, PA 16830
(814) 768-9911
P.O. Box 464
Ridgewau, PA 15853

CAPSEA (Citizens Against Physical
    Sexual Emotional Assault)
P.O. Box 267
Emporium, PA 15834
(814) 486-1227 office
(814) 486-1122 hot line

Erie County Rape Crisis, Inc.
125 West 18th Street
Erie, PA 16507
(814) 455-9414
1-800-352-7273

Hospitality House
P.O. Box 1436
Erie, PA 16512
(814) 454-8161 hot line
(814) 459-6440 legal

The YWCA of Greater Harrisburg
215 Market Street
Harrisburg, PA 17101
(717) 238-7273
1-800-654-1211

Survivors Resources
115 E. Hartford St.
Milford, PA 18337
(717) 296-2827

Women's Help Center, Inc.
809 Napoleon Street
Johnstown, PA 15901
(814) 536-5361

YWCA Sexual Assault Prevention
    and Counseling
110 North Lime Street
Lancaster, PA 17602
(717) 393-1735 office
(717) 392-7273 24-hour hot line

Sullivan County Victim Services
Box 272
Laporte, PA 18626
(717) 946-4215

Sexual Assault Resource &
    Counseling Center
    of Lebanon County
P.O. Box 836
Lebanon, PA 17042
(717) 272-5308

Women in Crisis
P.O. Box 155
Lehighton, PA 18235
(717) 377-0760 business
1-800-424-5600 24-hour hot line

The Alrise Network
P.O. Box 268
Lewistown, PA 17044
(717) 242-0715 office
(717) 436-2402 office
Both Mifflin/Juniata Counties
(717) 242-2444 hot line

Clinton County Women's Center
151 Susquehanna Avenue
Lock Haven, PA 17745
(717) 748-9509 hot line
(717) 923-2270 hot line
(717) 748-9539 office

Women's Services, Inc.
P.O. Box 637
Meadville, PA 16335
(814) 333-9766 hotline
(814) 724-4637 office

Lawrence County Women's
    Shelter/Rape Crsis Center
P.O. Box 1422
New Castle, PA 16103
(412) 652-9036

Laurel House
P.O. Box 764
Norristown, PA 19404
(215) 643-3150
1-800-642-3150

Victim Services Center of
    Montgomery County, Inc.
70 East Penn Street
Norristown, PA 19401
(215) 277-0932 business
(215) 277-5200 24-hour hot line

Family Service Rape
    Crisis/Domestic Violence
    Center
716 East Second Street
Oil City, PA 16301
(814) 677-4005 office
(814) 677-7273 hot line

Women Organized Against Rape
1233 Locust Street, Suite 202
Philadelphia, PA 19107
(215) 985-3333 24-hour hot line
(215) 985-3315 office

Allegheny County Center for
    Victims of Violent Crime
1520 Penn Avenue
Pittsburgh, PA 15222
(412) 392-8582 24-hour hot line
(412) 350-1975 office

Crisis Center North, Inc.
P.O. Box 101093
Pittsburgh, PA 15237
(412) 364-5556 hot line
(412) 364-6728 office

JCCEDA, Inc. Crossroads Project
105 Grace Way
Punxsutawney, PA 15767
(814) 938-3580 hot line
(814) 938-3302 community action

*Berks Women in Crisis
P.O. Box 803
Reading, PA 19603
(610) 372-9540 main #

CAPSEA, Inc.
Elk/Cameron Counties
P.O. Box 464
Ridgway, PA 15853
Elk County
(814) 772-3838 office
(814) 772-1227 hot line
Cameron County
(814) 486-1227 office
(814) 486-1122 hot line
(814) 772-9270 fax

AWARE, Inc.
P.O. Box 662
Sharon, PA 16146
(412) 981-3753 office

Victim's Resource Center, Inc.
109 West Central Avenue
P.O. Box 643
Titusville, PA 16354
(814) 827-0017 business
(814) 827-3472 24-hour hot line

The Care Rape Crisis Center
62 East Wheeling Street
Washington, PA 15301
(412) 228-2200 office
(412) 228-7208 office & sexual
    assault hot line

The Crime Victim's Center of
    Chester County, Inc.
236 West Market Street
West Chester, PA 19382-2903
(610) 692-7420 hot line

Domestic Violence Service Center
P.O. Box 1662
Wilkes-Barre, PA 18703
(717) 823-5834 business
(717) 823-7312 hot line
(717) 455-9971 hot line

Victims Resource Center
N. Hampton Corners Bldg.
85 South Main Street
Wilkes-Barre, PA 18701-1602
(717) 823-0766 business
(717) 823-0765 hot line

Access-York, Inc.
P.O. Box 743
York, PA 17405
(717) 846-5400
1-800-262-8444

Victim Assistance Center
P.O. Box 892
York, PA 17405
(717) 854-3131
1-800-422-3204

SOUTH CAROLINA

The Rape Crisis Center
    of the Low Country
P.O. Box 1919
Beaufort, SC 29901-1919
(803) 525-6699

Sistercare, Inc.
P.O. Box 1029
Columbia, SC 29208
(803) 765-9428

CASA
P.O. Box 912
Myrtle Beach, SC 19576

Tri-County CASA/Family Systems
P.O. Box 1568
Orangeburg, SC 29116-1568
(803) 531-6211
(803) 534-2272

SOUTH DAKOTA

Resource Center for Women
P.O. Box 41
Aberdeen, SD 57402
(605) 226-1212

Fall River Crisis Intervention Team
P.O. Box 995
Hot Springs, SD 57747
(605) 745-6070

YWCA Family Violence Program
17 5th Street, Southwest
Huron, SD 57350
(605) 352-2793
(605) 352-4952

Vermillion Coalition Against
    Domestic Violence
P.O. Box 144
Vermillion, SD 57069
(605) 624-5311

TENNESSEE

Kent C. Withers Family Crisis
    Center
2460 East Fifth Avenue

Knoxville, TN 37917
(423) 637-8000 24-hour hot line
(423) 673-3066 office

TEXAS

Crime Victim Crisis Center
P.O. Box 122
Abilene, TX 79605
(915) 677-7895 main #

Matagorda County Women's
    Crisis Center
P.O. Box 1820
Bay City, TX 77404-1820
(409) 245-9109 office
(409) 245-9299 hot line
1-800-451-9235

Bay Area Women's Center
P.O. Box 3735
Baytown, TX 77522
(713) 424-3300 office
(713) 422-2292 24-hour hot line

Rape Crisis/Victim Services
P.O. Box 1693
Big Spring, TX 79721-1693
(915) 263-3312 office
(915) 267-3626 office
(915) 263-1211 Scenic Mountain
    Medical Center 24-hr hot line

Denton County Friends of the
    Family
P.O. Box 640
Denton, TX 76202
(817) 382-7273 hot line
(817) 387-5131 office

Rape Crisis Program of the
    Women's Center of
    Jarrant County
1723 Hemphill Ave.
Fort Worth, TX 76110
(817) 927-2737 hot line

Family Crisis Center, Inc.
513 E. Jackson #207
Harlinger, TX 78550
(210) 423-9304 hot line & office

SAFE House
P.O. Box 1893
Huntsville, TX 77342
(409) 291-3369

Hill Country Crisis Council
P.O. Box 1817
Keriville, TX 78029-1817
(210) 257-7088 office
(210) 257-2400 hot line

Highland Lakes Family
    Crisis Center
P.O. Box 805
Marble Falls, TX 78654
(210) 693-3656
(210) 683-5600 24-hour hot line

Permian Basin Center
    for Battered Women
    and Their Children
P.O. Box 2942
Midland, TX 79702
(915) 683-1300
1-800-967-8928

Safe Space
Box 831

Newport, TX 37821
Unlisted

RAPE Crisis Center
P.O. Box 7741
Odessa, TX 79760
1-800-658-6779

Tralee Crisis Center
P.O. Box 2880
Pampa, TX 79066-2880
1-800-658-2796
(806) 669-1131 office

Hale County Crisis Center
P.O. Box 326
Plainview, TX 79073-0326
(806) 293-7273
(806) 293-9772
(806) 293-6273 hot line

Williamson County Crisis Center
211 Commerce, Suite 103
Round Rock, TX 78664
(512) 255-1212
1-800-460-SAFE

I.C.D. Family Shelter
P.O. Box 5018
San Angelo, TX 76902
(915) 655-5774
1-800-749-8631

Domestic Violence Prevention, Inc.
Rape Crisis Center
424 Spruce St.
Texarkana, TX 75501
(903) 793-4357
(903) 794-4000 office

Hope of South Texas
P.O. Box 2237
Victoria, TX 77902
(512) 573-5868
(512) 573-3600 24-hour hot line

Center for Action Against Sexual
    Assault
Community Services Bldg.
201 West Waco Drive, Suite 213
Waco, TX 76707
(817) 752-9330 business
(817) 752-7233 hot line

Montgomery County Women's
    Center
P.O. Box 8666
Woodlands, TX 77387-8666
(409) 441-7273
(713) 292-4338

UTAH

Center for Women &
    Children in Crisis
Box 1075
Provo, UT 84603
(801) 377-5500
(801) 374-9351

Rape Recovery Center
2035 South 1300 East
Salt Lake City, UT 84105
(801) 467-7273 24-hr hot line
(801) 467-7279 office
1-800-656-4673

YWCA Women in Jeopardy Program
322 East 300 South
Salt Lake City, UT 84111
(801) 355-2804

VERMONT

*Women's Rape Crisis Center
P.O. Box 92
Burlington, VT 05402
(802) 864-0555 office
(802) 863-1236 hot line

Sexual Assault Crisis Team
P.O. Box 1313
Five School Ave.
Montpelier, VT 05602
(802) 223-7755
1-800-639-2341

VIRGINIA

Alexandria Office On Women
110 North Royal Street, Room 201
Alexandria, VA 22314
(703) 838-5030 office
(703) 683-7273 hot line

TACTS
P.O. Box 1285
Annandale, VA 22210
(703) 237-0881
(703) 522-8858

The Crisis Center
P.O. Box 642
100 Oakview Avenue
Bristol, VA 24203
(540) 466-2312 hot line
(540) 466-2218 office

Sexual Assault Resource Agency
P.O. Box 6705
Charlottesville, VA 22906
(804) 977-7273 hot line
(804) 295-7273

Shelter for Help in Emergency
P.O. Box 3013
University Station
Charlottesville, VA 22903
(804) 293-6155 office
(804) 293-8509 hot line

Services to Abused Families, Inc.
P.O. Box 402
Culpeper, VA 22701
(540) 825-8876
(540) 349-0309

Kristin Little
RCASA
P.O. Box 1276
Fredericksburg, VA 22402
(540) 371-1666

Middle Peninsula-Northern Neck
    Community Services Board
P.O. Box 427
Gloucester, VA 23061
(804) 693-5068 administration
(804) 693-COPE hot line

CASA-Citizens Against Sexual
    Assault
P.O. Box 1473
Harrisonburg, VA 22801
(540) 432-6430 office
(540) 434-2272 hot line

Response Sexual Assault Support
    Services
253 West Freemason Street
Norfolk, VA 23510
(804) 623-2115 office
(804) 622-4300 24-hour hot line

YWCA Women In Crisis
253 West Freemason Street
Norfolk, VA 23510
(804) 625-5570
(804) 625-4248 shelter hot line

Women's Resource Center
    of the New River Valley
P.O. Box 306
Radford, VA 24141
(540) 639-9592 administration
(540) 639-1123 hot line

SARA-Sexual Assault Response &
    Awareness
Blue Ridge Community Services
1009 1st Street, Southwest
Roanoke, VA 24016
(540) 981-9352 24-hour hot line

Alternatives for Abused Adults
P.O. Box 1414
Staunton, VA 24402-1414
(540) 886-6800 office and crisis

Family Crisis Services
P.O. Box 487
Tazewell, VA 24651
(540) 988-5583

The Shelter
P.O. Box 14
Winchester, VA 22604
(540) 667-6466

WASHINGTON

Human Response Network
P.O. Box 337
Chekalis, WA 98532
(360) 748-6601

Domestic Violence/Sexual Assault
  Program
220 West 4th Avenue
Ellensburg, WA 98926
(509) 925-9861 office
(509) 925-4168 24-hour hot line

Providence Sexual Assault Center
P.O. Box 1067
Everett, WA 98206
(206) 258-1275 administration
(206) 252-4800

Emergency Support Shelter
P.O. Box 877
Kelso, WA 98626
(360) 425-1176 office
(360) 425-2500 hot line

King County Sexual Assault
  Resource Center
P.O. Box 300
Kewton, WA 98057
(206) 226-7273

Volunteers Against Violence
Route 1, Box 1450
Lopez, WA 98261
(360) 468-2749 main number

Safe Place
P.O. Box 1605
Olympia, WA 98507
(360) 786-8754 office
(360) 754-6300

Ferry County Community
  Services/Connections
470-1 Klondike Road
Republic, WA 99166

(509) 775-3341 daytime
(509) 775-3332 after hours

Catherine Booth House
P.O. Box 20128
Seattle, WA 98102
(206) 324-4943 24-hour hot line

The Family Violence Project
Suite 1414
710 2nd Avenue
Seattle, WA 98104
(206) 684-7770

Spokane Sexual Assault Center
South 7 Howard, Suite 200
Spokane, WA 99204
(509) 747-8224 office
(509) 624-7273 24-hour hot line

YWCA Alternatives to Domestic
  Violence
Carolyn Jones Morrison, MSW,
  ACSW
829 West Broadway
Spokane, WA 99201
(509) 327-9534 main number

*Lower Valley Crisis & Support
  Services
P.O. Box 13
Sunnyside, WA 98944
(509) 837-6689

Sexual Assault Crisis Center of
  Pierce County
Allenmore Medical Center
1901 South Union, Suite A-114
Tacoma, WA 98405

(206) 597-6424 answering service
  line
(206) 474-7273 answering service
  line

YWCA Women's Support Shelter
407 Broadway
Tacoma, WA 98402
(206) 383-2593 crisis
(206) 272-4181 YWCA Office

WEST VIRGINIA

Women's Resource Center
P.O. Box 1476
Beckley, WV 25802-1476
(304) 255-2559

Family Service of Kanawha Valley
  REACH Program
922 Quarrier Street, Suite 201
Charleston, WV 25301
(304) 340-3676
1-800-656-HOPE

Resolve Family Abuse Program
1114 Quarrier Street
Charleston, WV 25301
(304) 340-3554 main number
(304) 340-3549 hot line

Contact Huntington, Inc.
P.O. Box 2963
Huntington, WV 25729-2963
(304) 523-3447 office
(304) 523-3448 24-hour hot line

Family Crisis Center
P.O. Box 207
Keyser, WV 26726
(304) 788-6061 main number

Family Refuge Center
Box 249
Lewisburg, WV 24901
(304) 645-6334 main #

Stop Abusive Family
  Environments, Inc.
P.O. Box 234
Welch, WV 24801
(304) 436-8117 hot line
(304) 436-6181 office

Family Violence Prevention Program
1100 Chapline Street
Wheeling, WV 26003
(304) 232-0511
(304) 232-2748 hot line

Upper Ohio Valley Sexual Assault
  Help Center
P.O. Box 6764
Wheeling, WV 26003
1-800-884-7242 hot line
(304) 234-8519 hot line
(304) 234-1783 office

Tug Valley Recovery Shelter
P.O. Box 677
Williamson, WV 25661
(304) 235-6121 24-hour hot
  line/office
(304) 235-6167 fax

WISCONSIN

AVAIL, Inc.
P.O. Box 355
Antigo, WI 54409
(715) 623-5767 hot line
(715) 623-5177

Outagamie County Domestic
    Abuse Program
401 South Elm Street
Appleton, WI 54911
(414) 832-1666 24-hour crisis

Hope House
P.O. Box 432
Baraboo, WI 53913
1-800-584-6790 crisis

Family Services Associates
Sexual Assault Center
131 South Madison Street
Green Bay, WI 54301-4587
(414) 436-8899

Women's Horizons, Inc.
P.O. Box 792
Kenosha, WI 53141
(414) 652-1846 crisis

Menominee County
    Human Services Dept.
P.O. Box 280
Keshena, WI 54135
(715) 799-3861

Rape Crisis Center
128 East Olin Avenue
Madison, WI 53713
(608) 251-5126 office
(608) 251-7273 crisis

Stepping Stones Shelter, Inc.
P.O. Box 224
Medford, WI 54451
(715) 748-3795

HAVEN, Inc.
P.O. Box 32

Merrill, WI 54452
(715) 536-9563 business
(715) 536-1300 crisis

Green Haven Family Advocates
P.O. Box 181
Monroe, WI 53566
(608) 325-6489 office
(608) 325-7711 crisis

Oneida Domestic Abuse Program
P.O. Box 365
Oneida, WI 54155
(414) 869-4415 business
1-800-574-0187 24-hour hot line
(414) 869-1661 local

Sexual Abuse Services, Inc.
201 Ceape Avenue
Oshkosh, WI 54901
(414) 426-1460
(414) 722-8150
(414) 426-1460

Family Advocates, Inc.
P.O. Box 705
Platteville, WI 53818
348-3838 local
(608) 348-5995 business
1-800-924-2624 crisis

Safe Harbor
P.O. Box 582
Sheboygan, WI 53082
(414) 452-7640

Family Crisis Center
1616 West River Drive
Stevens Point, WI 54481
(715) 345-6511 office
1-800-472-3377 hotline

Help of Door County, Inc.
P.O. Box 319
Sturgeon Bay, WI 54235
(414) 742-8818
(414) 743-8818 crisis

Center Against Sexual or
    Domestic Abuse
2231 Catlin Avenue
Superior, WI 54880
(715) 392-3136

The Women's Center, Inc.
726 North East Avenue
Waukesha, WI 53186
(414) 547-4600 administration
(414) 542-6777 business
(414) 542-3828 24-hour hot line

The Women's Community
2801 N. 7th St., Suite 300
Wausau, WI 54403
(715) 842-7323 hot line
(715) 842-5663 office

Family Center, Inc.
531 10th Avenue, North
Wisconsin Rapids, WI 54495
(715) 421-1511

WYOMING

Self-Help Center
341 East E, Suite 135A
Casper, WY 82601
(307) 835-2814

SAFE Task Force, Inc.
350 City View Drive, #208
Evanston, WY 82930
(307) 789-3628 office
1-800-442-7233 hot line

SAFE Project
P.O. Box 665
Laramie, WY 82070
(307) 742-7273 office
(307) 745-3556 hot line

*Helpmate Crisis Center
302 North Main
P.O. Box 89
Lusk, WY 82225
(307) 334-3416 office
(307) 334-2608 24-hour hot line

FOCUS (Foundation of Caring,
    Understanding & Services)
P.O. Box 818
Newcastle, WY 82701
(307) 746-2748
1-800-459-2748

Carbon County COVE
P.O. Box 713
Rawlins, WY 82301
(307) 324-7071
1-800-442-8337

YWCA Support & Safe House
P.O. Box 1667
Rock Springs, WY 82902
(307) 382-6925 24-hour hot line
(307) 362-7674 office

Women's Center
P.O. Box 581
Sheridan, WY 82801
(307) 672-7471

Project Safe, Inc.
P.O. Box 8
Wheatland, WY 82201
(307) 322-4794

Appendix B

Where to Call for More Information

The following organizations provide information about wife rape.

For information on state laws, a state law chart (available for $3), speakers on wife rape, volunteer internships, and information/referrals on wife rape), contact:

Laura X, Director
National Clearinghouse on Marital and Date Rape
2325 Oak Street
Berkeley, CA 94708
(510) 524-1582

The subscription rate for the National Clearinghouse is $15 for individuals, $30 for organizations per year, and the subscription includes phone consultations at a cost of $7.50 per 15 minutes.

For those interested in receiving a brochure (English and Spanish are available) entitled *Stopping Sexual Assault in Marriage*, which addresses the problem of wife rape, women's rights, state laws, and where to get help, contact:

Center for Constitutional Rights
666 Broadway, 7th Floor
New York, NY 10012
(212) 614-6464

For a marital rape information packet and information on state laws ($25.00), contact:

National Center on Women and Family Law
799 Broadway, Room 402
New York, NY 10003
(212) 741-9480

. For lawyers who want legal information on wife rape and state legislation, contact:

Center for Constitutional Rights
666 Broadway, 7th Floor
New York, NY 10012
(212) 614-6464

For a variety of documents on wife rape, including scholarly literature, popular articles, court testimony, and legislative correspondence, contact:

Marital Rape Information
Women's Studies Library
University of Illinois
415 Library
Urbana, IL 61801
(217) 244-1024

For an information packet on wife rape, as well as information for starting wife rape support groups and training programs on wife rape for staff and volunteers ($2), contact:

Domestic Violence Project
P.O. Box 7052
Ann Arbor, MI 48107
(313) 995-5444

For information on wife rape and civil litigation, see *Domestic Violence Practice and Procedure*, by Friedricha Lehrman.
Clark, Bordman, and Callahan (1996).

Women who need assistance and are looking for referrals to local rape crisis centers and battered women's shelters (which may or may not have specific services for wife rape survivors) should see Appendix A, or contact:

National Coalition Against Domestic Violence
(303) 839-1852

or

Texas Council on Family Violence
1-(800)-799-SAFE

or

National Victim Center
1-(800) FYI-CALL

Appendix C
State Law Chart

T he following information was adapted from a chart prepared by the National Clearinghouse on Marital and Date Rape, Berkeley, California, March, 1996. The clearinghouse has been campaigning for almost 20 years for changes in legislation and continually updates the chart for accuracy. For information on obtaining an updated chart, please send $3.00 to the National Clearinghouse on Marital and Date Rape, 2325 Oak St., Berkeley, CA 94708 (see Appendix B).

On July 5, 1993, wife rape became a crime in all 50 states. In 17 states and the District of Columbia, there are no exemptions from rape prosecution granted to husbands under the law. This is also the case on federal lands. An asterisk (*) indicates the lack of such an exemption. However, 33 states still have some exemptions from prosecuting husbands for rape. Ironically, in most of these states, a husband is exempt when he does not have to use force because his wife is vulnerable (e.g., mentally or physically impaired, unconscious) and is legally unable to consent. In five states—Connecticut, Delaware, Iowa, Minnesota, and West Virginia—the privilege to rape is extended to cohabitors. In Delaware, the privilege is extended to dates.

Alabama	Arizona
Alaska	Arkansas

California
Colorado*
Connecticut
Delaware
Florida*
Georgia*
Hawaii
Idaho
Illinois
Indiana*
Iowa
Kansas
Kentucky
Louisiana
Maine
Maryland
Massachusetts*
Michigan
Minnesota
Mississippi
Missouri
Montana*
Nebraska*
Nevada

New Hampshire
New Jersey*
New Mexico*
New York*
North Carolina*
North Dakota*
Ohio
Oklahoma
Oregon*
Pennsylvania
Rhode Island
South Carolina
South Dakota
Tennessee
Texas*
Utah*
Vermont*
Virginia
Washington
West Virginia
Wisconsin*
Wyoming
District of Columbia*
Federal lands*

Appendix D
Researching Wife Rape

W ithin the field of sociology there is a growing body of confessional literature in which researchers attempt to explain how they conducted their research and the problems they encountered. Given the sensitive nature of my subject matter, I feel compelled to do the same. In this appendix, I will try to share with the reader how I collected data for this book, the obstacles I encountered, and the ethical issues I confronted.

Several methods were used to conduct this research, including participant observation, content analysis, survey, and most significant, in-depth interviews. Much of the information for this book is taken from extensive field notes I accumulated during my 18 months of participant observation at a rape crisis center and a battered women's shelter. I chose to study these agencies because I felt they were the types of organizations that survivors of wife rape would most likely contact for help. Having read Russell's (1990) criticism that those involved in the anti-rape and anti-wife abuse movements often neglect the issue of wife rape, I was interested in learning how two individual organizations manage the problem.

Access to these organizations was granted on the basis of my previous affiliation with each program. I participated in a 40-hour training program required by the state to become a crisis counselor. I was a former employee of the rape crisis center and continued to be a volunteer at the time of my data collection. My status at the battered women's shelter varied during my data collection from employee to volunteer. As a member of each organization, I worked with battered women and sexual assault survivors in a variety of capacities, from providing crisis intervention and emotional support to helping women and their children find adequate housing. I also was afforded great opportunities to observe the daily workings of each agency. I attended meetings and training sessions for new employees and volunteers and observed how staff members interacted with the women who sought their services.

My observations were supplemented by my content analysis of client files (for a 2-year period), made available to me while I constructed a list of potential respondents to interview about their experiences of wife rape. It is important to note that these lists were treated with great caution—they remained at the agency, and the identity of each woman remained confidential. Also, in analyzing files, I focused only on questions such as how a woman was referred to the agency, length of stay, and so forth; no identifying information was collected. Doing this analysis was important for framing my understanding of each agency's formal and informal policies regarding the problem of wife rape.

An important source of data for this book was a questionnaire I sent to 1,730 service providers listed in two directories: *Sexual Assault and Child Sexual Abuse: A National Directory of Victim/Survivor Services and Prevention Programs* (Webster, 1989) and the 1991 *National Directory of Domestic Violence Programs,* compiled by the National Coalition Against Domestic Violence.[1] Of those sent, 621 were completed and returned, a response rate of about 36%. In this survey, respondents were asked specific questions about their mission statement, training programs, and the types of services they provide to survivors of wife rape. For a copy of the survey, please see Appendix E.

In addition to these methods, I interviewed 37 service providers from the rape crisis center and battered woman's shelter where I studied. The interviews with staff members lasted from about 1 hour to 2 1/2 hours and were based on a series of open-ended questions. I spoke with each staff member about her training in wife rape and her perceptions of and experiences with wife rape survivors. My hope was that by conducting these interviews, I would come to learn how workers frame the issue of wife rape and how they manage this population on a daily basis.

Although each of the above-mentioned methods of data collection was important in framing the problem of wife rape, the richest sources of information were the stories shared with me by 40 survivors of wife rape.

All of the women interviewed had been raped by their partners at least once, and all had contacted a women's agency for support. The vast majority (35) of these women had contacted either the rape crisis center or battered women's shelter with which I was working. However, five of the women had contacted another rape crisis center or battered women's shelter for support but were referred to me by others with knowledge of my work.

Any woman who called the rape crisis center or battered women's shelter and mentioned (either voluntarily or in response to questions about their expereinces of violence) that her partner had forced her to have sex, made her do things sexually she was uncomfortable with, or raped her was a candidate for participation in this study. I attempted to contact each woman who met one or more of these criteria and who had called either agency during a 2-year period. How potential participants were contacted differed at each organization.

At Refuge (the battered women's shelter), a staff member was chosen (for her sensitivity) by myself and the director to contact women who might be willing to participate in this study. This employee explained my credentials as a member of the organization, the purpose of the research (to understand women's experiences of wife rape), and the types of questions I would ask. Each woman was assured that her continued contact with Refuge was in no way contingent upon her decision to participate in the study and that she could stop the interview at any time. The staff member who was involved in this process expressed no trepidation about contacting women for this study and was quite diligent in her efforts to find women who were willing to share their experiences with me.

At WASA (Women Against Sexual Assault—the rape crisis center), the president of the organization initially provided an employee who fulfilled largely the same role as the Refuge staff member, and most interviews with WASA clients were completed in this manner. However, during my data collection, the president informed me that she did not have the woman-power to spare and that I would have to contact survivors of wife rape on my own. To promote their confidentiality, I called women only from the agency telephone, and I did not remove any identifying information about them from the organization's files. When I was successful in reaching a woman, I tried to be as noncoercive as possible and to let her know that WASA services would continue regardless of whether she participated in my study. In many instances, staff members played an important role by alerting me when they were working with a survivor of wife rape, and I commonly solicited their help in asking for the woman's participation.

The interviews with survivors of wife rape contained a series of open-ended questions and ranged from 1 hour to 4 hours in length (see Appendix E for a copy of the interview guide). The average length was 2 hours. I asked each woman about her relationship with her partner, past experiences of violence, and any sexual or other types of abuse inflicted by her partner. Because I was interested in how women define their experiences of rape and the role that agencies play in this defining process, I spoke with each woman at length about her perceptions of the violence and how these perceptions changed with time. I also asked each woman about her contact with service providers and how she would evaluate the services she had received.

I attempted to contact each woman after her interview to check on her emotional well-being and to see if she had additional concerns, questions, or information regarding the study. With several women, follow-up interviews were conducted, and additional information about their contact with service providers and their progress in healing was gathered.

Obstacles to This Study

The most significant obstacle I faced was locating women to interview about their experiences of wife rape. Ultimately, I was successful in interviewing 7 women from WASA, 21 from Refuge, 7 who had contacted both agencies for support, and 5 women who were helped by another women's agency. However, I was not successful in speaking with every survivor of wife rape who had contacted these agencies during this 2-year period. There are several reasons for this.

First, I was not able to interview every woman who called Refuge for help. Given the nature of wife rape, it is not surprising that women who had been sexually abused and sought shelter at Refuge were not easily located. Women who are fleeing abusive husbands are not likely to be at the same address that they used when they first contacted the agency, and many had also changed their phone numbers or chosen to have unlisted numbers. Furthermore, it is not unusual for those women who leave the shelter to be transient for a few years. Without spousal support, many of those women were forced to accept public assistance and often moved from one housing project to another.

For the women who contacted WASA, a common problem was that they called anonymously, and their names, addresses, and phone numbers were not documented in the files. Thus, the vast majority of phone numbers and addresses were inaccurate.

A second problem emerged when women were still involved with their abusive partners. Obviously, it was difficult to reach these women and ask for their participation in the study. Frequently, a male voice would answer the phone and I was forced to hang up or pretend to have a wrong number.[2]

If I was successful in reaching these women, they were not always willing to discuss their experiences for a variety of reasons. Several were fearful that their husbands would learn they were talking to a researcher about the sexual abuse. Another woman initially agreed to speak with me but later changed her mind because she and her (new) partner thought it would be difficult for her to dredge up "old memories." A few women did not want to talk because they said they were not rape victims. One woman I reached said, "I've never called WASA—I've never been raped." For whatever reasons, this woman, whose file indicated that she had contacted the agency on several occasions, did not want to discuss her experiences.

The final problem I encountered was meeting with all of the women who were sheltered at Refuge. Several women agreed to participate in the study but were asked to leave (because of drug or alcohol use) before I had an opportunity to interview them. Two other women indicated they had been raped by their partners, but before they were even asked to participate, they left the shelter and did not leave forwarding addresses. Thus, we see that there were a variety of obstacles to overcome in my collecting data on this subject.

Ethical Considerations

I faced three major ethical dilemmas while doing this research, and it is important to briefly address each one. As other researchers (Renzetti & Lee, 1993) have noted, there are particular difficulties associated with conducting research on socially sensitive topics. I have argued (Bergen, 1993) that wife rape is a sensitive topic primarily because of the potential emotional and/or physical threat that speaking to a researcher about these experiences poses to the women involved. In addition, such research is sensitive in that it delves into the intimate, private sphere of the marital bedroom and calls into question historical understandings of the marital contract. Studying a sensitive topic such as wife rape raises important ethical considerations. Although there are many ways to resolve these questions, my work has been guided by my commitment to feminist principles and models of research (Duelli Klein, 1983; Maguire, 1987).

The most significant ethical considerations stem from the fact that as a researcher, I was asking women to share their most intimate and painful experiences with me. Thus, it was essential that each woman's confidentiality be ensured and that I minimize the emotional effects of the interviews for the women involved.

I tried to protect the confidentiality of the wife rape survivors in several ways. First, I conducted all of the interviews and transcribed all of the tapes myself. After I completed the transcriptions, the tapes were destroyed and the written transcripts were kept in a locked file. The women were identified on the transcripts not by name but only by number. A list containing the corresponding names and numbers was kept in a safe deposit box. Furthermore, when writing about individual cases, I changed each woman's name and deleted any identifying information that might put her at risk.

A second set of ethical questions involved the possibility that the interviews would be emotionally disturbing for some women. I felt that my training and experiences as a rape crisis counselor and battered women's advocate helped to make me sensitive to the experiences these women endured. However, I took several precautions to reduce the risk of inflicting emotional harm on these women.

First, I tried to be particularly cautious both that my questions were sensitive and that they allowed women to fully express their own thoughts. For this reason, I tried to ask open-ended questions and encouraged each woman to tell her own story in her own way. To further reduce emotional distress, I tried to convey, prior to the interview, that some of the information might be difficult to discuss.[3] Furthermore, on one occasion, I stopped the interview because a woman became extremely upset and was crying uncontrollably.[4]

Following each interview, I tried to alleviate any negative emotional impact. I encouraged each woman to seek help if she experienced flashbacks, nightmares, or other adverse reactions. I also provided each woman with literature containing information about wife rape, a contact number for me, and a list of counseling services in the community. At Refuge, each woman was told about the counseling staff, which was at her disposal 24 hours a day if she wanted to talk. As I indicated previously, I also tried to contact each woman 1 or 2 days after the interview to check on her emotional well-being and to see if she had any further questions or concerns. Through these measures, I tried to minimize the emotional impact the interviews had on the survivors of wife rape.

A final ethical requirement with this type of research is that each woman must freely give her informed consent to participate in the project. As I explained earlier, it was important that a Refuge staff member talked with each potential participant prior to her meeting with me. Both the director of Refuge and I felt that it was necessary for the women in shelter to understand that their staying at Refuge and receiving help was in no way contingent upon their agreement to participate. At WASA, it was more difficult to avoid these ethical considerations because I was the person who contacted several of the women regarding their participation. In the few cases that I was successful in reaching women, I emphasized that the decision to participate was solely their own and that they would continue to receive services regardless of their decision.

Although the ethical questions involved in doing this research initially appeared daunting, I tried to use great caution and sensitivity in contacting women and speaking with them about their experiences. Most women were either grateful that someone was legitimating their experiences or hopeful that their stories would help others. In general, the women seemed pleased to be involved in this project, and many were grateful for the opportunity to talk about a serious problem that had influenced their lives.

Notes

1. Although these directories are dated, at the time the survey was generated, there were no more current listings available. Thus, these directories were supplemented by many lists that were provided to me by individual state coalitions.

2. The use of caller identification boxes makes telephone contact potentially dangerous for wife rape survivors, advocates, and researchers. In some areas, the

telephone company can provide battered women's shelters and rape crisis centers with "untraceable" numbers to alleviate this problem.

3. I also discussed the consent form with each woman and explained her right to end the interview at any point or to refuse to answer any question.

4. At this time, we discussed the dynamics of what was going on, and I reminded her that she could end the interview at any time. After several minutes and a cup of tea, this woman continued with the interview. Following the interview, I told her about support services available to help her. I also called her the next day; she seemed relatively calm and told me that she was happy to have spoken with me.

Appendix E

Research Instruments

Survey of Services for Wife Rape Survivors

Please answer each of the following questions by checking the box(es) which corresponds to the response that best identifies your services, or by filling in the blank spaces where appropriate.

1. Official title of person completing the survey

2. Which of the following best describes the service which you provide to women?
   [ ] Shelter
   [ ] Rape crisis center
   [ ] Combination battered women's shelter/rape crisis center
   [ ] Hot line (nonresidential services only)
   [ ] Other (please specify)

3. Do you do outreach to victims of marital rape?
   [ ] Yes
   [ ] No

3a. If you do not do outreach to marital rape victims, please check the primary reason why.

[ ] Marital rape is not a problem in the community

[ ] We don't receive many calls from marital rape victims

[ ] We have a shortage of staff and/or volunteers

[ ] We do not differentiate between marital rape and other types of violence

[ ] Marital rape victims don't require special services

[ ] Other (please specify)

3b. If you do outreach to marital rape victims, please check each category that describes your efforts.

[ ] Brochures which focus specifically on marital rape

[ ] Brochures which mention marital rape

[ ] Presentations to the community specifically on marital rape

[ ] Presentations to the community in which marital rape is mentioned

[ ] A media campaign specifically focused on marital rape

[ ] Other (please specify)

4. If you have a screening procedure for clients, do you make it clear that you provide services to victims of marital rape?

[ ] Yes

[ ] No

[ ] Does not apply/we have no screening procedure

[ ] Does not apply/we do not accept marital rape victims

5. Are women routinely asked about their experiences of marital rape during the screening process?

[ ] Yes

[ ] No

[ ] Does not apply/we have no screening process

6. How are women identified as victims of marital rape?

[ ] Initial intake forms (screening process)

[ ] They self-identify

[ ] Individual counseling

[ ] Group counseling

[ ] We do not identify victims of marital rape

[ ] Other (please specify)

6a. If women are routinely asked about marital rape, what questions are they asked?

7. What services does your agency provide to victims of marital rape?
   [ ] Hospital accompaniment
   [ ] Legal service accompaniment
   [ ] Crisis intervention
   [ ] Shelter
   [ ] Individual counseling
   [ ] We provide no services to marital rape victims
   [ ] Other (please specify)

8. Do you provide a support group specifically for victims of marital rape?
   [ ] Yes
   [ ] No

8a. If you do not provide a support group for marital rape victims, are marital rape victims welcome in support groups for battered women?
   [ ] Yes
   [ ] No

8b. If yes, please describe how you make it clear that victims of marital rape are welcome in the support group.

9. What percentage of your clientele are victims of marital rape?

9a. What is this number based on?
   [ ] Agency statistics
   [ ] Self-reports from victims
   [ ] Knowledge of the current population receiving services
   [ ] Best guess
   [ ] Other

10. Which of the following groups receive training specifically on the topic of marital rape?
   [ ] Staff
   [ ] Volunteers
   [ ] Training is not provided on this topic

11. If training is provided on marital rape, what does the training include?
   [ ] Legal rights of marital rape victims
   [ ] Identifying marital rape victims
   [ ] Emotional reactions of victims to marital rape

[ ] Counseling marital rape victims
[ ] Resources for marital rape victims
[ ] Other (please specify)

12. What is the official mission of your agency?

13a. Is providing services to victims of marital rape included in the mission of the agency?
[ ] Yes
[ ] No

13b. If providing services to marital rape victims is not included in your mission, please check the primary reason why.
[ ] Marital rape is not a problem in the community
[ ] The agency does not receive any calls from marital rape victims
[ ] Shortage of staff and/or volunteers
[ ] Shortage of space available
[ ] Another agency is primarily responsible for handling marital rape victims
[ ] Marital rape victims require different services than we can provide
[ ] Other (please specify)

14. Which type of agency in your community is responsible for handling the largest number of marital rape victims?
[ ] This agency
[ ] A rape crisis center
[ ] A battered women's shelter
[ ] Don't know
[ ] Other (please specify the name of the agency)

15. Which of the following services do you provide to husband rapists?
[ ] Individual counseling
[ ] Support groups
[ ] We do not provide services to husband rapists
[ ] Other

16. If you would like your services included in a resource guide, please mark an X here and complete the identifying information below.
Name of your agency:
Mailing address:
Relevant phone numbers:

Thank you for completing this survey. Please place the survey in the enclosed stamped envelope and drop it in the mail.

Interview Guide for Survivors of Wife Rape

Background

A.1. Can you tell me about the events which brought you here? [Probe: What events led you to call the shelter?]

A.2. Did you contact any other agency besides this one?
  a. What did they tell you?
  b. How did they treat you?

Relationship

Now I want you to tell me about your relationship. Feel free to stop me at any time, and if you feel uncomfortable with a question, let me know.

B.1. How many times have you been married? [Probe: If more than one marriage: I would like you to concentrate on the relationship which led you to come here.]

B.2. How long were you with your partner?

B.3. a. What first attracted you to him? [Probe: What did you find appealing about him?]
  b. How long did you know each other before you got married?
  c. What were the main reasons you got married at that time?

B.4. What were your expectations about marriage? [Probe: What did you think it would be like to be married to him; did you expect your marriage to be like that of your parents?]

B.5. a. Prior to your marriage, were you ever sexually or physically assaulted?
  b. Can you tell me what happened?
  c. What was your age?
  d. How long did it go on?
  e. How did it end?

B.6. a. What was sex with your husband like?
  b. Who initiated intercourse?
  c. How often did you regularly have sex?

B.7. Did you ever have any unwanted sexual experiences with your husband? [Probe: Did your husband ever force you to have sex against your will?]

B.8.   a. What happened when he forced you for the first time?

      b. How did you react? [Probe: Did you try to resist?]

      c. Do you remember what you were thinking at the time?

B.9. What did you think after the first incident? [Probe: Did you think, "He raped me?"]

B.10. How often did he force you?

B.11.   a. Did you notice any patterns to his forcing you?

      b. Did he use drugs or alcohol before he forced you?

      c. Did you have arguments before each incident?

      d. Did the violence increase when you became pregnant?

B.12. Can you tell me about one time that stands out in your mind? [Probe: What's significant about that time?]

B.13. Was your husband ever physically violent with you, other than the sexual assault? [Probe: Did your husband ever hit you?]

B.14.   a. Do you feel the forced sex was part of the physical violence?

      b. Was the physical abuse separate from the forced sex?

      c. Which did you find the hardest to handle, the physical or sexual abuse?

B.15. Do you think of your experience as "rape"? [Probe: Do you think of your husband as a rapist?]

B.16.   a. When did you see it as such?

      b. After how many incidents?

B.17. Did your feelings about what was going on change over the course of the relationship?

B.18. Why do you think that your partner acted that way? [Probe: Why did he force you to have sex?]

B.19.   a. Did your husband ever look at pornography?

      b. Do you see any relationship to the forced sex?

B.20. a. How much effect did the forced sex have on your relationship?

   b. Your life? [Probe: Emotional, physical, sexual effects?]

B.21. Do you plan to file a restraining order against your husband? [Probe: Can you tell me why you want (do not want) a restraining order?]

B.22. a. What contact do you have with your husband now?

   b. Do you ever think about getting back together with your husband? Why or why not?

   c. Would you ever consider going back if he changed?

Network

C.1. Do you know of anyone else who has had similar experiences?

C.2. a. Did you ever speak to anyone about your experiences? [Probe: Did you talk to a family member or a friend?]

   b. Why did you choose to tell that person?

   c. What was his or her reaction?

   d. How did you feel after talking to him/her?

   e. If not, why not?

C.3. Have you told your family or friends why you left your husband?

C.4. Do you feel that they have been supportive of your decision? [Probe: Do you feel that they understand why you left?]

Organization

D.1. What made you decide to call here? [Probe: What triggered your decision to call a shelter?]

D.2. How do you like it here?

D.3. Why do you think most of these women are here? [Probe: What caused others to seek shelter?]

D.4. a. Have you spoken with other women here about your experiences?

   b. What was their reaction?

   c. Were they supportive?

D.5. a. Have you spoken to any staff members about the forced sex?

     b. Did they ask you specifically about the forced sex?

     c. Did you feel comfortable discussing your experiences with them?

D.6. How can the staff be the most helpful to you?

D.7. Do you feel like you have special needs because of the sexual abuse? [Probe: Do you feel like you are different from the other women here?]

D.8. What is your biggest concern right now? [Probe: Are you most concerned about your safety, legal issues, finding a place to live, money, etc.?]

D.9. What are your plans for the future?

D.10. Is there anything you would like to tell me that's important that I have not asked about? Are there any questions you would like to ask me?

References

Adams, C. (1993). I just raped my wife! What are you going to do about it, pastor? In E. Buchwald, P. Fletcher, & M. Roth (Eds.), *Transforming a rape culture* (pp. 57-86). Minneapolis, MN: Milkweed.

Alsdurf, J., & Alsdurf, P. (1989). *Battered into submission*. Downers Grove, IL: InterVarsity Press.

Article 120, Uniform Code of Military Justice, *Manual for Courts-Martial,* paragraph 45 (1984).

Astor, G. (1974). *The charge is rape.* Chicago: Playboy Press.

Augustine, R. I. (1991). Marriage: The safe haven for rapists. *Journal of Family Law, 29,* 559-591.

Barshis, V. (1983). The question of marital rape. *Women's Studies International Forum, 6,* 383-393.

Bergen, R. K. (1993). Interviewing survivors of marital rape: Doing feminist research on sensitive topics. In C. M. Renzetti & R. M. Lee (Eds.), *Researching sensitive topics* (pp. 197-211). Newbury Park, CA: Sage.

Best, J. (1990). *Threatened children: Rhetoric and concern about child-victims.* Chicago: University of Chicago Press.

Bidwell, L., & White, P. (1986). The family context of marital rape. *The Journal of Family Violence, 1,* 277-287.

Blumer, H. (1971). Social problems as collective behavior. *Social Problems, 18,* 298-306.

Blumstein, P., & Schwartz, P. (1983). *American couples: Money, work, and sex.* New York: William Morrow.

Bowker, L. (1983). *Beating wife beating.* Lexington, MA: Lexington Books.

Bowker, L. (1986). *Ending the violence.* Holmes Beach, FL: Learning Publications.

Browne, A. (1987). *When battered women kill.* New York: Free Press.

Browne, A. (1993). *Report of the Council on Scientific Affairs* (I-91). Washington, DC: Council on Scientific Affairs.

Brownmiller, S. (1975). *Against our will: Men, women, and rape.* New York: Simon & Schuster.

168

Campbell, J. C. (1989). Women's responses to sexual abuse in intimate relationships. *Health Care for Women International, 10,* 335-346.

Campbell, J. C., & Alford, P. (1989). The dark consequences of marital rape. *American Journal of Nursing, 89,* 946-949.

Campbell, J. C., Poland, M., Waller, J., & Ager, J. (1992). Correlates of battering during pregnancy. *Research in Nursing and Health, 15,* 219-226.

Cavanagh, C. (1978). *Battered women and social control.* Unpublished manuscript.

Dobash, R. E., & Dobash, R. (1979). *Violence against wives: A case against the patriarchy.* New York: Free Press.

Drucker, D. (1979). The common law does not support a marital exemption for forcible rape. *Women's Rights Law Reporter, 5,* 2-3.

Duelli-Klein, R. (1983). How to do what we want to do: Thoughts about feminist methodology. In G. Bowles & R. Duelli Klein (Eds.), *Theories of women's studies.* London: Routledge & Kegan Paul.

Edwards, S. S. M. (1989). *Policing "domestic" violence.* London: Sage.

Ferraro, K., & Johnson, J. (1983). How women experience battering: The process of victimization. *Social Problems, 30,* 325-338.

Finkelhor, D., & Yllö, K. (1985). *License to rape: Sexual abuse of wives.* New York: Holt, Rinehart, & Winston.

Frieze, I. (1983). Investigating the causes and consequences of marital rape. *Signs: Journal of Women in Culture and Society, 8,* 532-553.

Frieze, I. H., & Bulman, R. J. (1983). Theoretical perspectives for understanding reactions to victimization. *Journal of Social Issues, 39,* 1-17.

Gelles, R. (1977). Power, sex, and violence: The case of marital rape. *The Family Coordinator, 26,* 4.

Gelles, R. (1988). Violence and pregnancy: Are pregnant women at greater risk of abuse? *Journal of Marriage and the Family, 50,* 841-847.

Gordon, M., & Riger, S. (1989). *The female fear.* New York: Free Press.

Gornick, J., Burt, M., & Pittman, K. (1985). Structure and activities of rape crisis centers in the early 1980s. *Crime and Deliquency, 31,* 247-268.

Griffin, M. (1980). In 44 states, it's legal to rape your wife. *Student Lawyer, 9,* 1.

Groth, N. (1979). *Men who rape.* New York: Plenum.

Gusfield, J. R. (1981). *The culture of public problems: Drinking-driving and the symbolic order.* Chicago: University of Chicago Press.

Hanneke, C., & Shields, N. (1985, October). Marital rape: Implications for the helping professionals. *Journal of Social Casework,* pp. 451-458.

Hanneke, C., Shields, N., & McCall, G. J. (1986). Assessing the prevalence of marital rape. *Journal of Interpersonal Violence, 1,* 3.

Hawkins, J. (1991, April). Rowers on the River Styx. *Harvard Magazine,* pp. 43-52.

Herman, J. (1981). *Father-daughter incest.* Cambridge, MA: Harvard University Press.

Hilgartner, S., & Bosk, C. (1988). The rise and fall of social problems: A public arena model. *American Journal of Sociology, 94,* 1.

Hoff, L. (1990). *Battered women as survivors.* London: Routledge.

Joffe, C. (1986). *The regulation of sexuality.* Philadelphia: Temple University Press.

Kelly, L. (1988). *Surviving sexual violence.* Minneapolis: University of Minnesota Press.

Kelly, L. (1990). How women define their experiences of violence. *Psychology of Women Quarterly, 36,* 114-131.

Kinsey, A., Wardell, C., Pomeroy, B., & Martin, C. D. (1953). *Sexual behavior in the human female.* Philadelphia: University of Pennsylvania Press.

Koss, M. P., & Harvey, M. (1991). *The rape victim.* Newbury Park, CA: Sage.

Loseke, D. (1987). Lived realities and the construction of social problems: The case of wife abuse. *Symbolic Interaction, 10,* 229-243.

Loseke, D. (1992). *The battered woman and shelters: The social construction of wife abuse.* Albany: State University of New York Press.

Loseke, D., & Cahill, S. (1984). The social construction of deviance: Experts on battered women. *Social Problems, 31,* 297-310.

Maguire, P. (1987). *Doing participatory research: A feminist approach.* Amherst: The Center for International Education, School of Education, University of Massachusetts.

Malamuth, N. M., & Check, J. V. (1985). The effects of aggressive pornography on beliefs in rape myths: Individual differences. *Journal of Research in Personality, 19,* 299-320.

Martin, D. (1976). *Battered wives.* San Francisco: Glide Press.

Matthews, N. (1995). Feminist clashes with the state: Tactical choices by state-funded rape crisis centers. In M. Marx Ferree & P. Yancey Martin (Eds.), *Feminist organizations: Harvest of the new women's movement* (pp. 291-305). Philadelphia: Temple University Press.

Mills, T. (1985). The assault on the self: Stages in coping with battering husbands. *Qualitative Sociology, 8,* 2.

National Clearinghouse on Marital and Date Rape. (1995). 1995 state law chart. Berkeley, CA: Author.

National Directory of Domestic Violence Programs. (1991). Denver, CO: National Coalition Against Domestic Violence.

NiCarthy, G. (1986). *Getting free.* Seattle:, WA: Seal Press.

Pagelow, M. (1984). *Family violence.* New York: Praeger.

Pagelow, M. (1992). Adult victims of domestic violence. *Journal of Interpersonal Violence, 7,* 87-120.

Peacock, P. L. (1995). Marital rape. In V. Wiehe & A. Richards (Eds.), *Intimate betrayal* (pp. 55-73). Thousand Oaks, CA: Sage.

Renzetti, C. (1992). *Violent betrayal.* Newbury Park, CA: Sage.

Renzetti, C., & Lee, R. (1993). *Researching sensitive topics.* Newbury Park, CA: Sage.

Resnick, H., Kilpatrick, D., Walsh, C., & Vernonen, L. (1991). Marital rape. In R. Ammerman & M. Herson (Eds.), *Case studies in family violence* (pp. 329-353). New York: Plenum.

Rose, V. M. (1977). Rape as a social problem: A by-product of the feminist movement. *Social Problems, 25,* 75-89.

Rubin, L. (1976). *Worlds of pain.* New York: Basic Books.

Russell, D. E. H. (1990). *Rape in marriage.* Bloomington: Indiana University Press.

Saunders, D. G., & Size, P. B. (1986). Attitudes about woman abuse among police officers, victims, and victim advocates. *Journal of Interpersonal Violence, 1,* 25-42.

Schechter, S. (1982). *Women and male violence.* Boston: South End Press.

Schneider, J. W. (1985). Social problems theory: The constructionist view. *Annual Review of Sociology, 11,* 209-229.

Shields, N., & Hanneke, C. (1983). Battered wives' reactions to marital rape. In R. Gelles, G. Hotaling, M. Straus, & D. Finkelhor (Eds.), *The dark side of families.* Beverly Hills, CA: Sage.

Smith, M. D. (1994). Enhancing the quality of survey data on violence against women: A feminist approach. *Gender and Society, 8,* 109-128.

Sonkin, D. (1987). *Domestic violence on trial.* New York: Springer.

Stacey, W., & Shupe, A. (1983). *The family secret.* Boston: Beacon.

Straus, M., Gelles, R. J., & Steinmetz, S. K. (1980). *Behind closed doors: Violence in the American family.* New York: Anchor/Doubleday.

Thompson-Haas, L. (1987). *Marital rape: Methods of helping and healing.* Unpublished manuscript.

Turetsky, J. (1981, Fall). Marital rape and the law. *Woarpath,* pp. 4-11.

Walker, L. (1979). *The battered woman.* New York: Harper & Row.

Webster, L. (1989). *Sexual assault and child sexual abuse: A national directory of victim/survivor services and prevention programs.* Phoenix, AZ: Oryx Press.

Weingourt, R. (1985). Wife rape: Barriers to identification and treatment. *American Journal of Psychotherapy, 39,* 2.

Wertheimer, L. (Host). (1992, April 22). *All things considered.* Washington, DC: National Public Radio.

Whatley, M. (1993). For better or worse: The case of marital rape. *Violence and Victims, 8,* 29-39.

Wiehe, V., & Richards, A. (1995). The problem. In V. Wiehe & A. Richards (Eds.), *Intimate betrayal* (pp. 1-8). Thousand Oaks, CA: Sage.

X, Laura. (1994). A brief series of anecdotes about the backlash experienced by those of us working on marital and date rape. *The Journal of Sex Research, 31,* 151-153.

Index

About the Author

Raquel Kennedy Bergen is Assistant Professor of Sociology at St. Joseph's University in Philadelphia, Pennsylvania. She is also a crisis counselor for battered and sexually abused women. She has written several articles on wife rape, including "Surviving Wife Rape: How Women Define and Cope with the Violence," published in *Violence Against Women.*